brilliant

managing
your team
through
change

PEARSON

At Pearson, we believe in learning – all kinds of learning for all kinds of people. Whether it's at home, in the classroom or in the workplace, learning is the key to improving our life chances.

That's why we're working with leading authors to bring you the latest thinking and best practices, so you can get better at the things that are important to you. You can learn on the page or on the move, and with content that's always crafted to help you understand quickly and apply what you've learned.

If you want to upgrade your personal skills or accelerate your career, become a more effective leader or more powerful communicator, discover new opportunities or simply find more inspiration, we can help you make progress in your work and life.

Pearson is the world's leading learning company. Our portfolio includes the Financial Times and our education business, Pearson International.

Every day our work helps learning flourish, and wherever learning flourishes, so do people.

To learn more, please visit us at **www.pearson.com/uk**

brilliant

managing your team through change

Richard Newton

PEARSON

Harlow, England • London • New York • Boston • San Francisco • Toronto • Sydney
Auckland • Singapore • Hong Kong • Tokyo • Seoul • Taipei • New Delhi
Cape Town • São Paulo • Mexico City • Madrid • Amsterdam • Munich • Paris • Milan

PEARSON EDUCATION LIMITED

Edinburgh Gate
Harlow CM20 2JE
United Kingdom
Tel: +44 (0)1279 623623
Web: www.pearson.com/uk

First published 2015 (print and electronic)

Pearson Education is not responsible for the content of third-party internet sites.

ISBN: 978–1–292–06360–7 (print)
        978–1–292–06361–4 (PDF)
        978–1–292–06362–1 (ePub)
        978–1–292–08109–0 (eText)

British Library Cataloguing-in-Publication Data
A catalogue record for the print edition is available from the British Library

Library of Congress Cataloging-in-Publication Data
A catalog record for the print edition is available from the Library of Congress

10 9 8 7 6 5 4 3 2 1
18 17 16 15 14

Cover design by David Carroll
Print edition typeset in 10/14pt by 3
Printed in Great Britain by Henry Ling Ltd, at the Dorset Press, Dorchester,
Dorset

NOTE THAT ANY PAGE CROSS REFERENCES REFER TO THE PRINT
EDITION

This book is dedicated to those friends who across the changes life brings, I have lost touch with, whether by accident, as a result of bad choices, or through laziness. I wish you well.

Contents

About the author

Richard Newton is a consultant, programme manager and author. He has over 25 years' experience in business projects, focussing on organisational change programmes. Through his company, Enixus Limited, he has worked worldwide for a wide variety of major organisations. He regularly supports businesses in improving their capabilities to deliver projects and change. Richard is a popular speaker on project- and change management-related topics. He frequently runs seminars, workshops and speaks at conferences.

Richard is the author of 10 other books, which have been translated into 16 languages. His books cover various aspects of managing projects, achieving goals and delivering change. They can be grouped broadly under the theme of *getting things done* – for individuals, teams or organisations. In 2013, Richard's *The Management Book* won the CMI's management book of the year award. More about his writing can be found at **www.changinghats.co.uk**.

Richard has degrees in Mechanical Engineering, Economics and Philosophy. He is a member of the Change Management Institute, the Association of Project Managers, the Institute of Business Consulting, the Society of Authors and the Royal Society of Philosophy.

Publisher's acknowledgements

The publishers are grateful to the following for permission to reproduce copyright material:

Figure 7.3 reprinted with the permission of Taylor & Francis Books UK and Scribner Publishing Group, a division of Simon & Schuster Inc from *On Death and Dying* by Dr Elisabeth Kubler-Ross. Copyright © 1969 by Elisabeth Kubler-Ross; copyright renewed © 1997 by Elisabeth Kubler Ross. All rights reserved.

In some instances we have been unable to trace the owners of copyright material and we would appreciate any information that would enable us to do so.

Introduction

Another book, in fact another book about change management. At this point you may be feeling a little sceptical. After all, there are hundreds of books on change out there. Is there really a role for another book on change? Yes. I am certain there is for two reasons: most books ignore a key audience and they do not talk to the messy reality of organisations.

I have made four assumptions about the reader of this book. The first is that you are a team leader in an organisation of some complexity – that could be a business, a not-for-profit or part of the public sector. Your team is not made up of other managers, but operates at the coal face of the organisation. Your team consists of people doing the daily work the organisation needs to get done. The second assumption is that you need to drive, guide and facilitate your team through change. This book will help you to do this. My third assumption is that you want to improve your change management skills. You see it as an important part of your capabilities – essential for your job today and for your developing career as a manager. The advice in this book focusses on, but goes a few steps beyond, team change. My final assumption is that you work in an imperfect organisation. Textbook theory of ideal organisations is helpful, but practical advice based in reality is better. Your organisation is imperfect – it does not suddenly become perfect when change initiatives are started.

If these assumptions are true – this book is for you.

Although the primary intended audience is team leaders, this book will appeal to a wider readership. There is much for the senior manager here as well – to help you guide those who work for you through the changes they must lead. There is also material that will help change management professionals. Their role is often that of coaching and supporting managers through change programmes. The best way to do this is to see change from their viewpoint, which this book does.

The missing audience

Many change books miss or underplay one of the most important participants in change: the typical team leader in a complex organisation. Many books are aimed at the executive level. These have grand and often exciting titles about leading change. Some are aimed at the person who has to coordinate the change – a change leader or project manager. Others discuss the individual's personal journey through change.

These are important topics, but they miss one critical audience. Large organisations are built from teams. These teams typically have some form of team leader. This book is aimed at those line managers, team leaders and anyone who has a role in running a team. That team can have 5, 50 or 500 members. Irrespective of size, the team leader needs to drive some form of change with that team.

Change in teams is often a part of a wider organisational change. Such change is built up from individuals responding to change and accepting (or rejecting) it. But just thinking top down about change from the level of the whole organisation or bottom up from the viewpoint of individuals misses the very specific nature of team change and the challenges of the team leader in guiding this change. It's like creating a sandwich without worrying about the filling!

This book is a result of a set of key observations I have made during years of working on change programmes. I have worked as a team leader having to implement change, as a programme manager running change programmes, and as a consultant supporting organisations and their line managers through change. As I write this book I am working with two organisations in different continents providing support and guidance to their change programmes.

My observations start with the knowledge that team leaders can be the greatest barrier to change or they can be the lynchpin of success for a change programme. Further observations include the awareness that team leaders rarely are seen as the key asset in delivering change, in spite of being instrumental to it. Lastly, I conclude that many team leaders have to drive change initiatives without sufficient support or training. This seems particularly common for managers at the start of their careers.

> team leaders can be the greatest barrier to change or they can be the lynchpin of success

Change programmes and the language of change management are increasingly ubiquitous. We've all heard the mantra 'there is no constant but change'. Team leaders can be highly pressurised during change programmes, trying to balance three, often contending, pressures: helping their team through change, trying to continue to deliver the day-to-day work while changing, and their own personal experience of the change. And yet, given all of this, I often find that team leaders are the least trained people when it comes to change management. In this book I set out to start to rebalance this.

The messy reality of organisations

I want to address a different audience, and I want to do this in a different way from other change management books. I want to take account of the messy reality of most organisations. None of us work in that textbook idealised organisation with perfect strategy, processes and resources.

Team leaders work in the real world. Theory is interesting, but it is the application of theory to reality that matters. There is some underpinning theory in this book, but mostly it sets out to give practical and pragmatic advice. I take a realistic, warts and all view, of what it is like to work in a major organisation. I try to be honest. Be wary of the snake oil salesman promising you a cure to all your change problems. There are no silver bullets, but there are techniques and approaches which will reduce risk and make your journey smoother than it would otherwise have been. I will give you a balanced view of the different and often conflicting forces a team leader experiences during change programmes. I do not pretend the experience is always easy or pleasant, but I will show you that it does not need to be a nightmare!

There is one other thing I want to do. That is to increase your self-sufficiency and resilience. During a change programme you should be able to rely on the wider organisation for support. But sometimes the painful truth is that the rest of the organisation will let you down. Your boss may communicate something unhelpful, the strategy may be unclear or non-existent, HR may not deliver what you expect, your peers may create challenges for you, and annual pay rises and bonuses may not support you in driving the behaviour you want. These are examples of the hundreds of issues that form the reality of most team leaders' work.

resilience in the face of organisational flaws is key to a successful and happy career as a manager

These are not examples of deliberate or terrible management and leadership. It is just the reality that we are all human, and sometimes people you think should know and perform better don't do so. There are limits to how self-sufficient you can be, otherwise you would not be part of a larger organisation. But I want to help you to take what's best from your organisation and survive its flaws. All organisations have them! Resilience in the face of organisational flaws is key to a successful and happy career as a manager.

Team leaders and change

Change throws up challenges for many people in different roles across the organisation. Team leaders have their own set of issues to deal with during change. Four are worth highlighting:

1   From a team leader's perspective one issue is the unpredictability of change. Unpredictability in itself is not a problem. Unpredictability is just what life is like sometimes. The issue for the team leader is dealing with unpredictability in the face of the requirement to make and keep commitments, such as delivering projects in predicted timescales, or maintaining operational performance while changing.

2   A second issue is your personal workload. Times of change can place significant pressures on team leaders. You may find yourself having to find time to guide change in an already busy schedule.

3   The third issue is dealing with different, sometimes conflicting viewpoints of change. How can you align the needs of the organisation, the needs of your team and your own personal needs?

4   The fourth issue is your skills and capabilities to pull together all the activities needed to successfully deliver change, and to guide your team through the process of changing. The aim of this book is to help you achieve this, in the face of the previous three difficulties.

Let's elaborate on the first three of these issues a little more.

Change is concerned with people, and people will respond to change in unpredictable ways. Managers have to deal with each of their team members' individual responses to change. Such responses can be positive or negative, explicit or hidden, rational or emotional. Responses to change cannot be assessed or analysed on a spreadsheet. Some can be predicted, but in the end it is only by working with, listening to and observing your team that you will find out their real responses. And it is the real response you must deal with, not your prediction. The most common word associated with response to change is resistance, but not all responses will be simply resistance and even if they are, resistance takes many forms. While change activity needs to be planned, it must also be handled flexibly as the reality of the situation and people's responses to change unfold.

Leading a team through change requires effort and focus, but you will not be let off your day job of managing your team. In times of change, a manager can become heavily loaded. One mistake managers sometimes make is to underestimate the effort involved in a change. Another is to focus too little on performing the tasks necessary to achieve a change – and in doing this to forget the day job and for team performance to drop. With the right planning and approach it is possible to find the right balance and mitigate the risk of being overloaded.

Some kinds of change are not only hard work, but are also emotionally demanding. While many changes are benign for everyone involved – some may have negative consequences for some of your team members. Dealing with situations such as redundancies or negatively perceived role changes can be emotionally draining and stressful. Again though, with the right approach and planning you will be able to deal with this.

A big challenge for a line manager is the conflicting perspectives you have to deal with during a change. You are part of your team, so you may share the team's perspectives about a change. But you are also part of the management and need to represent the enterprise's view of the change. Sometimes these views conflict. Finally, you have your own perspective about whether a change is a good or a bad thing for you personally. As a team leader you are not just another team member. Therefore you must not fall into the trap of avoiding anything contentious or unpopular because you associate too closely with your team. On the other hand, you must not simply enforce the organisation's viewpoint. Without taking the time to understand the team's needs and perspectives you will not be able to act as a true leader. If you don't understand and try to balance these viewpoints, achieving change will be hard and sometimes impossible.

Leading change throws up big challenges. But do not panic. There are many simple, practical tools and techniques that combine planning and structure with flexibility and responsiveness that will help you succeed. In this book we will explore some of these that will make your life as a change leader easier and reduce the risks associated with undertaking change.

How to use this book

This is a short book and I hope you will find it packed full of tips and techniques that reassure and help you. When you finish it I want you to be both more confident and more effective at guiding your team through change. A book is inherently a linear structure, but unfortunately change management is not a subject that is fully decomposable into a perfect linear structure of do step 1, then step 2 and finish with step 3. I have to make cross-references between earlier and later chapters. I try to minimise these as it disrupts the reading, but I don't want to give you the impression that there is a perfect linear ordering to change. The order I have chosen for the chapters seems the most logical to me – but don't interpret that as an instruction to work solely in this order.

Read this book however you prefer. You can read it end-to-end or dip in here and there. Best of all is to scan it quickly to understand the lay of the land, then read it end to end, and finally keep it on your desk to pick out those bits and pieces you need when you are working on a change initiative with your team.

Whichever way you choose, good luck!

CHAPTER 1

Understand the journey and your role in it

You want to, or have to, undertake a change. My first advice is to stop and think. In this chapter I share some ideas to help inform your thinking and shape your way of approaching change. This chapter also sets the background for change, provides some definitions and challenges a few of the myths of change.

Experiencing change is often compared to a journey, and this is a metaphor I will come back to time and again in this book. It's a well-known and slightly tired metaphor, but it is one I will stick with because it is a very good one for the experience of change.

The journey is about to begin. The very first step in this journey is to understand what you are about to undertake. Let's start by briefly outlining the shape of the journey we will be discussing in this book. Next I will talk about the main players in every organisation and any change: teams, managers and leaders. Then we'll move onto some other fundamentals of change.

The shape of the journey

A significant part of this book will be spent discussing the best way to make your team's change journey. It is important to consider this journey in its wider context, as there are many factors outside of an individual change initiative which will have an effect on how successful that journey is. This is the perspective I have taken in creating this book.

For me there are four stages (see Figure 1.1) which team leaders need to consider:

1 ***The departure:*** the important point will be that making a smooth journey depends on how you start and set your direction as well as how you manage the change itself. This is covered in chapters 2 and 3.

2 ***The change journey itself:*** this is the core material of the book, and is discussed in chapters 4, 5, 6, 7 and 8.

3 ***Business as usual:*** as a team leader you not only have to deliver the change, critically you need to maintain business as usual performance in your team. That is doing the day job your team normally does. Change can have an effect on your daily work. This is examined in chapters 5 and 6.

4 ***The arrival:*** a journey is no use unless you arrive and manage to stay where you want to get to. Also, as experienced managers know, the end point of one journey is usually the starting point for the next. These points are explored in chapter 9.

With this context set, let's go back to talking about the main players in this journey.

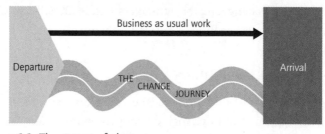

Figure 1.1 The stages of change

Teams, managers and leaders

The word 'team' has different meanings to different people. For some, when they hear 'team' they think about sports and a team that sets out to win a game. For others it is a set of people who have some common goal or objective. Those interested in organisational behaviour explore teams in comparison to other structures such as groups.

I am largely going to ignore this complexity as I do not think it adds much to the day-to-day management challenge of running a team as part of an organisation. I will use what I see as an intuitive sense of a team. A team is simply a unit in the hierarchy of an organisation. Teams are the building blocks of organisations. It's not a particularly exciting definition, but it does the job and relates well to most peoples' actual experience of the word 'team' being used at work.

The team may have some common area of activity such as the order management team, or share a temporary goal, such as with a project team. The team may have a specific functional skill set, such as the finance team, or could be responsible for a common stage in a business process, such as the customer services team. On the other hand, a team may be created for a completely pragmatic reason such as that all the people work in one location. Teams exist for all these reasons and more. Some reasons for putting a team together are better than others. Some theorists may not consider such a unit of people working together to be a 'proper' team. Yet in normal work most of such units would be called teams, rightly or wrongly. And in this book I am dealing with normal work, not academic discussions.

Teams experience change frequently. In fact, the very structure of the team is often the focus of a change. Changes are initiated to reconfigure teams that have been put together for a specific reason, into organisational units structured on a different basis.

For instance, teams organised along functional skills may be reorganised around business processes.

As a result of these team reconfigurations, one of the most common complaints people make is 'we are constantly changing around here'. When you scratch below the surface of this complaint it is often a grumble that 'we are constantly reorganising around here. Can't someone senior just make up their mind as to how to organise us and leave it at that?' More bluntly, what people mean when they say this is 'our leaders are idiots who keep on experimenting but don't know the right answer, which they should, given what they are paid'. Sometimes this belief has a grain of truth in it, but often it is a result of poorly managed and poorly explained change rather than the wrong change or a badly designed change.

In this book I am going to assume you are not responsible for organisational design at the top level of the organisation. I envisage that to a significant extent, for better or worse, you have the team you have. You cannot just decide to run a different team. You can reconfigure the resources you have to some degree, but there will be a wide set of organisational policies and principles which limit your freedom as to precisely how you organise the people in your team. There is also the reality of budgets and headcount limits that constrain your freedom. You may have built the team, or you could have inherited it when you got your job as a team leader. Whatever is the exact nature of your team, it is your interaction with this team as their team leader that is the focus of this book.

The typical situation in a team is that there is some interdependence between the functions of different team members that makes it more efficient or effective for them to work as one group. Sitting in the middle of this team is someone who performs a management role. Job titles vary – team leaders, line managers, departmental heads and so on. This is all a rather long-winded way of explaining and stressing the point that organisations are made up of teams, and those teams have team leaders.

There is growing interest in self-organising teams without team leaders. Some of the emerging concepts are exciting, but they are outside the scope of this book to explore. I caution you not to get carried away with thoughts of the universal death of the line manager. The claims are premature, if not simply wrong. The reality is that large organisations, built up from teams and line managers, are here to stay for quite some time yet.

A welcome change in the past few decades has been the move away from the detailed directive style of historic management, to the adoption of what is often portrayed as a leadership style. The leadership movement has significantly improved the way organisations are run. Unfortunately, there is often an almost revolutionary fervour to the strongest leadership advocates – 'we want leaders and not managers'. Like many revolutions, the original drive for the revolution has a solid basis in need, theory and practice. But the idea that there is simply no longer any need for managers belies the truth about working in most organisations and the maturity of those organisations. There are also cultural aspects to consider as to the appropriate balance between leadership and management.

There seems to be no simple consensus as to what leadership is versus management. Drucker famously made the statement that 'Management is doing things right; leadership is doing the right things'. If we just focus on

> good change management is about doing the right thing... in the right way

this definition then one can easily argue that leadership is paramount, but management still remains important. Good change management is about doing the right things, but it is also about doing them in the right way. I see no conflict in trying to develop both leadership and management skills.

Leadership and change make good partners, but I want to differentiate between roles and styles. I see leadership and management as different styles or approaches used to guide teams. We discuss both as we go through this book. I will take it as a given that the person running the team be called a 'manager' or a 'leader' – it's just a job title! Here I mostly refer to you as *the team leader*. (And for those fixated on separating leaders from managers, with this job title the irony is greatest. Ask most people what a team leader is – and I expect many will say 'a type of manager'.) To be successful, a leader/manager needs to be able to flow between management and leadership styles of interaction with their team.

Change

Change is a ubiquitous topic in modern management. Again, I want to use another simple and intuitive explanation. A change happens when someone does something differently – they stop doing one thing in a particular way and start doing it in another way. Put differently, if at the end of a change initiative no one is doing anything differently then it has not been successful. This definition is so broad that it could encompass a huge variety of events and undertakings in organisations – and that is my point. Change is not just spoken about as ubiquitous, it is ubiquitous.

Businesses launch new products and services all the time. Organisations grow bigger, smaller and relocate. Companies run performance improvement initiatives. Corporations reorganise, outsource and then insource work. Departments restructure teams and modify their procedures. Improved IT systems, new machinery and other technology is implemented. The list of possible changes is probably endless.

The critical point about change is that it concerns human behaviour. The result of change is that team members will be working in a different way. This may mean delivering different outputs or accepting different inputs, using new tools, processes or systems. It can mean that the team has fewer or more members. It may be that the team leader is managing (or leading) in a different way. I don't want to, and I don't think I need to, limit change to too tight a definition. I think we all get the idea.

The metaphor of a journey comes into its own when we think about change. A team starts in state A, a change is undertaken and the team ends in state B. The journey is often thought of as the journey from state A to state B. But that journey starts earlier and finishes later than this description implies. The journey includes the preparations done before starting to travel between A and B, and includes the work once a team has arrived at B to ensure it stays there and does not somehow drift back to A. This final point is normally referred to as sustaining change. Sustaining change is an important topic I will discuss in this book.

Why change?

One question when talking about change is *why bother*? Change uses up scarce resources, is risky in terms of operational performance and often ends up unsettling team members. Submitting to such high costs and risks deserves a good explanation.

There are two simple answers to the *why bother* question. The first is that often there is no choice. There are social, economic, technological, environmental and competitive forces that organisations have to respond to. The second is that change often offers a prize in terms of business benefits or performance improvements which seems to justify taking the risk and the cost.

Experience shows that often the given justification for change was developed with rose-tinted glasses and a lack of a full understanding of the risks associated. As a result the business history books are full of stories of failed change. Even so, change is here to stay. Look around and observe any successful organisation.

Below that success lies regular change. One of the key reasons for exploring change is to ensure your changes end up in this latter category.

Interests

It's not hard to convert generic reasons for change into the goals to achieve from a specific change. But take care in doing this: goals are relative. Different people, even when they have chosen to do the same thing, often have different goals. When it comes to organisational change many of the people who experience it have not chosen to undertake change. It is imposed on them by others. When you want to understand the goals of change, it is pertinent to ask 'whose goals?'

Usually when we talk about the goals of change initiatives we think in terms of the goals of the organisation as a whole. If you think about this in any detail you soon realise that this is hardly helpful, as the organisation is a fairly abstract concept. We could debate for a long, long time what we mean by 'in the organisation's interest'. I think there is usually a rough-and-ready, good-enough sense of something being done for an organisation's interest. If you work for a business this is something like the shareholder's interest, if you work for the public sector this maybe the interest of society, and if you work for a not-for-profit organisation this is usually a reflection of the interests of a group of stakeholders that not-for-profit organisation represents.

The concept of an 'interest' is worth considering because one of the reasons achieving sustained change is difficult is that people resist it. Resistance to change is a reflection of a difference in interests. The classic situation is when a change is in the interest of an organisation but not in the interest of employees. Why wouldn't you resist something that was not in your interest? Resistance is not some

> resistance is not some terrible monster – it is perfectly natural and understandable

terrible monster. It is perfectly natural and understandable. It is something you will certainly have to deal with.

Successful change

From your perspective as a team leader, and given the variety of interests to consider, what is the measure of success for a change? I think this is best explored with an example with conflicting interests. An extreme example, but one that most managers will have to deal with at some time in their career: a change which results in redundancies. Not all changes require redundancy, but some of the most difficult to implement do. They are often the most uncomfortable for a team leader to be responsible for.

In the situation of redundancy the organisation's benefit could be in terms of a reduced salary bill or changing skills by replacing existing staff with new staff with different skill sets. Your team members' interests are usually not to lose their jobs. But if a process of redundancy is inevitable then their practical interest becomes to lose jobs in the least damaging way. This normally means with good severance packages and help with finding new roles. There are many other factors to consider. Some of the organisation's and team members' interests will conflict, some will not.

Following redundancy, I have seen situations in which good friendships are damaged and individuals leave with a grudge and will bad-mouth the organisation and their previous team leader at every opportunity. You may be surprised that I sometimes have sympathy for these people. There are some who will never be pleased, but often bad responses derive from badly managed change. On the other hand, I have seen situations in which people leave an organisation, shake a manager's hand and while they may not want to leave, agree they have been well treated and go with respect for the organisation and their team leader.

From the team leader's perspective this example should illuminate your goal: to try and find the right balance between organisational and team member interests. Where those interests conflict, not to take a one-sided view of only your team's or only your organisation's interests; where one party is a loser, to try and find ways to mitigate this loss; where it is possible to align interests, to go the extra mile to achieve this. Your hands will be tied to some extent by the organisation's needs, rules, procedures and policies, but you can at least target this sort of goal.

brilliant tip

It's not all bad news!

Change brings many good things into organisations, such as new roles, development and learning opportunities, new products and services, promotions and organisational growth. I will quite often refer to redundancy in this book. It's not because I am obsessed by it or am a thorough pessimist. I much prefer working on changes that deal with growth and development. But redundancy is common in modern organisations. It is often the test case for how good your change management skills are and how mature you are as a leader. It does not just affect the individuals who are made redundant, but also the rest of the team members and your relationship with them. It is almost certainly something you will have to deal with in your career. If you can deal with the difficult stuff, then I am fairly sure you can also deal with the good stuff!

The vehicles of change

The most obvious and popular vehicle of change is a project or a programme. A classic example is a project to deliver a new IT system which results in a new way of working on a business process, which in turn delivers some business benefits such as greater efficiency or reduced costs. Projects and project management are well-proven tools in the delivery of change.

While all business projects deliver some change (or at least should do if they are worthwhile), it is not true that all changes are delivered by projects. A change may be delivered by the day-to-day management approach taken in an organisation – for example, by the styles of management communications, adapting leadership behaviour and often modifications to the performance management systems used in an organisation. There are more specialised tools used to drive specific forms of change in organisations. Six sigma and lean now have a long track record of driving ongoing change in organisations and improving operational performance levels.

Whichever vehicle is used, whether it is a specific project, a management initiative or tweaking the performance management system, it is important to be clear about the difference between the approach, the deliverables, the benefits and a sustained change. The approach is the way you go about achieving the change. The deliverables are things you create to facilitate the change – for instance new processes or improved IT systems. The benefits are the gains your team and the organisation achieve as a result of using those deliverables. A sustained change is the situation in which a change is achieved and is maintained, and as a result benefits should continue to be achieved. The latter is most relevant as change has an unfortunate tendency to unravel with individuals reverting to work in previous ways. (This is discussed more in chapters 7 and 9.)

One of the main tools that has developed is the practice of change management. There seems to be no single universal definition of change management. For many years change management has been a label applied to a bundle of theories and approaches which have only one thing in common: they are used on change initiatives and someone, somewhere claimed they were a part of change management.

Change management is coming of age and is moving from a relatively fluid and imprecise state to a more defined and mature discipline (see Appendix 3). If you are engaged regularly in change it is well worth thinking about developing skills in different change management tools. This book is a good place to start and should be enough to guide you as a team leader. But it is a short book and cannot be exhaustive. If change management interests you, then there is plenty more advice and help available.

brilliant tip

Project or initiative?

As there are many different ways of delivering change, rather than plumping for the word project or programme, which comes naturally to me, I will mostly use the less specific word initiative in the rest of this book. That's not because I don't like projects. I am a big fan of project management. It's just I don't want to lose sight of the fact that not all changes are delivered as part of a project.

The experience of change

I am intrigued by people who say 'I love change', 'I embrace change' and so on. I am always sceptical. My observation is that when people say things like this, they generally mean 'I am quite happy helping other people to change' or 'I accept change in certain areas of my life that I am willing and choose to change in'. I think few people accept change willingly, irrespective of what part of their life it affects. There are many areas of our lives where most of us crave stability – and dislike change.

Often, we have no choice but to change. I don't want to get into a philosophical debate about the level of voluntarism when it comes to change, but all the evidence points to one thing. All of us will experience multiple changes throughout our lives. Work and the organisations we work in account for a significant chunk of this change we will experience. Given this we might as well learn to deal with it in the best way possible, and even embrace it if we must. As a grounding for this I would like to make a few very general points about the experience of change.

First, as a team leader you cannot fully control change. The change journey is unpredictable, and you will not be able to fully plan for every eventuality. You have to be willing to learn and adapt as the change unfolds. Rarely do change journeys go in perfectly straight lines. This does not mean you should not plan. Being prepared is still the best option, and a plan is essential for successful change.

There are lots of weary and unexciting arguments about management versus leadership – delivering change takes both. Change undoubtedly will call on your leadership skills in setting the example for the team when you yourself are not always certain of what to do next. But it will also build on the day-to-day management processes you have put in place (see chapter 2 for more on this topic).

As a team leader, you probably won't always get the support you need and deserve from everyone else in the organisation in implementing change. If you are well prepared you may be ahead of others in the organisation in delivering change. Some of your colleagues will behave unhelpfully and probably should know better. But see this as an opportunity to shine rather than as a major problem. Learning to be resilient in the face of organisational weaknesses will serve your career well.

You cannot make people change. People choose to change, or choose not to change. There is always a choice at work. In extremis, this

> you cannot make people change

choice may be realised by people opting to leave an organisation.

That may be sad, but is easy to deal with. Often people exercise their choices in more subtle ways – individuals will try to ignore, avoid or undermine change. This is much harder to deal with. Don't get overly obsessed by this point as most people, most of the time, are quite reasonable about adapting to change. But you should never assume that just because you say or even mandate a change it will happen. In modern society, mandating change is one of the least successful ways to achieve sustained change.

Finally, the end point of change is rarely stability, or if it is, it is very brief. The end point of a change initiative is usually the start of the next change. That is not to say there are not times when the ongoing changes are minor evolutionary, continuous improvement and relatively straightforward to adapt to. However, more radical reorganisations, new processes, new tools and so on are a normal part of the regular cut and thrust of work.

> the end point of change is rarely stability

Your role in change

Change can stress the ambivalent and sometimes conflicting roles of the team leader. From outside the team, the team leader is a member of the team. From inside the team, the team leader is an outsider representing the interests of the organisation. As a team leader you are a member of your team and also a member of your boss's team. Skilful managers balance the demands of these viewpoints. Change can bring the contrasting viewpoints into conflict.

During change, your role as a team leader has five main aspects. You can think of these as different hats you must wear as a team leader during change. (The thought that you need to adopt different hats during change is why my blog site is called *changing hats*.) The hats are:

1 ***Represent the interests of the organisation to the team:*** the first role of a manager during a change is to

guide the team through the process of change so the organisation can achieve the goals it set out when it started this change. This is covered mainly in chapter 7, but also in chapters 3, 4 and 8.

2 *Represent the interests of the team to the organisation:* as well as looking inward at the team from the viewpoint of the organisation and the management hierarchy, a team leader needs to look outward from the team to the rest of the organisation. Your team needs to be able to work with the change, and sometimes this requires you to try and influence the ideas being imposed onto your team to reflect your team's interests. This is discussed in chapters 3, 4 and 7.

3 *Maintain normal roles and performance:* normally, even though a change is ongoing, you and your team have to continue to 'do the day job'. An organisation cannot stop its work just because it is implementing a change, and as a result none of the teams can either. This is covered in chapter 6.

4 *Go through the change yourself:* as a member of the team you will often be personally affected by the change. Your personal journey through change can require significant energy and thought trying to protect your own interests and career aspirations. This is touched on in chapter 7.

5 *Lead the change:* you have a choice whether you directly act as the agent driving the change on a day-to-day basis or if you delegate this to one of your team members. But either way, if the change is to be successful you have a role acting as a focal point and evangelist for the change. As a team leader leading change in a team, you should think of your role in two ways. The first way is the task of ensuring the activities that are required to make the

change happen are managed in a structured way (see chapters 4–8). The second way is about creating an environment in your team in which change can take hold (see chapters 2, 7 and 8).

The leadership team of the organisation you work in share aspects 1, 3 and sometimes 5 (depending on the change) with you, but typically are less engaged in aspects 2 or 4. Your team members share aspects 2 and 4, but are less worried about aspects 1, 3 or 5. Only the team leader typically experiences aspects 1, 2, 3, 4 and 5 *simultaneously*. And this is why your role in change is often the hardest. This book is here to help you weave your way as you journey through 1, 2, 3, 4 and 5. Many managers before you have succeeded in doing this – experience shows it is perfectly possible. Experience also shows it can be demanding, especially if you do not approach it in the right way.

There is a sixth aspect to change which I will discuss in the next chapter, and that is not concerned with individual changes, but with developing the basis in your team for change (see Figure 1.2). Many of the things you do as a manager, or choose not to

Figure 1.2 The six change hats of a team leader

do, will ease or hinder every change you undertake. If you work in a normal organisation in which change is ubiquitous, it is well worth getting this basis right. Even when you are not undertaking change, the way you manage and lead your team will set the basis for how easy or difficult change will be when it does occur.

Establishing yourself as a change leader

The most interesting and exciting thing about change, and the one that can sometimes feel overwhelming, is how broad a set of skills it will call on from you. When change is going on in your team you are like the conductor of an orchestra. The team will look to you for leadership and will need you. Together, you make the music. Yet at the same time your role is quite different. You must rely on team members playing their instruments while you wield the baton. You need to make sure each instrument contributes the right sound, while not playing an instrument yourself!

You will need to provide thought, direction and strategy. You will have to show organisational awareness and an understanding of the bigger picture of the organisation beyond your team. You will need to be able to structure and plan – and then drive progress. Change will call on your knowledge of process, systems and HR. You must become people-aware and sensitive to the mood of the team. You will draw on your relationship-building skills and rapport. And you will need to show expertise in communications.

This may all seem a tall order. Don't worry. No one expects you to be perfect at any of these, and we all have our strengths and weaknesses. If you are self-aware and open to feedback, change will help you understand your strengths and weaknesses

change will help you understand your strengths and weaknesses in each area in each area. Change will help you develop these skills. Change may occasionally seem like a fight for survival. Work at it and you will find a key leadership tool to help you thrive.

What's in it for you?

There is an inherent tension in being a team leader which you must balance. At its best this is a creative tension that produces a powerful synthesis of viewpoints. At its worst this can be an emotionally draining and personally damaging tension (see Figure 1.3). The tension results from the three interests you must juggle:

- If you accept the team leadership role then an obligation goes with this to participate in the management of the company and do what is right for the organisation. Sometimes this may not be in your team's interests.
- If you expect your team members to follow up and treat you as their leader then you have an obligation to them as well to try and support their interests. This may conflict with the organisation's interests.
- You are human and have your own interests. These will sometimes align with neither your organisation's nor your team's interests.

(Even this is a simplification as in reality team members may have quite varied interests, and you may have to consider the interests of other stakeholder groups such as suppliers and customers.)

As a result of this tension one question you may sometimes find yourself asking is: why should I comply with the demands of change? This is the 'what's in it for me' question.

Change can create a lot of work, not all of which you will get thanks for. But it has benefits. First, and most starkly, you may keep your job, simply because keeping your job requires you to follow the organisation's change strategy. Secondly,

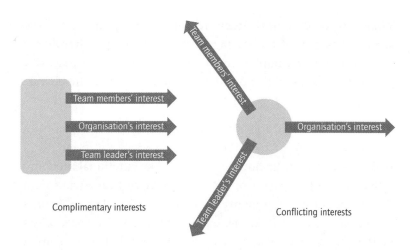

Figure 1.3 The team leader's tension in change

constructively working towards a change goal will be less stressful than being difficult about it. Thirdly, you will learn by engaging in change and practising change management skills. Being able to lead change is increasingly a requirement of managers. There are more career opportunities for those who have a proven track record with change. For your own sanity and stress levels, and for your personal career development, try to embrace change and be willing to learn from the experience. Fourthly, change is often in your team members' interests. What's good for the organisation is often good for them too. Change initiatives also help them acquire new skills and ensure their roles have longer-term relevance.

This would all be much easier for me to advocate if all changes were well thought through and in the interests of both the organisation and the team you lead. In reality, the interest of the organisation and your team members will sometimes clash. Additionally, I would be lying if I said all the changes you will be asked to do will actually be right for your organisation. Your senior leaders will sometimes be mistaken and, very occasionally, deluded about the benefits of a particular change.

What can you do in this situation? You can put your head in the sand, act as part of the management team, comply thoroughly with decisions and implement the change come what may. But you may sense an ethical problem if you really think the change is wrong. I am afraid there is no simple answer.

If you feel you must object to a change then you need to put a case forward to your boss. Develop your argument clearly and make it fact-based. It should not sound like emotional moaning – that will not help you or your cause. If you can structure a strong fact-based argument to show why the change is misplaced you may well influence the direction. I advise, when taking this course of action, to differentiate between fighting a worthwhile and winnable battle with pointless valour. In a perfect world executives and senior managers would always respond positively to a well-reasoned argument. In many organisations this will happen, but it would be naive to think it always will.

Choose your battles carefully. It is rarely worth damaging your career on a point of principle, if in doing so you have no effect on the course of change and its impact on your team. On the other hand, if you have a successful track record in delivering change, when you raise concerns, you are more likely to be listened to.

brilliant recap

In this chapter I have set the scene for change, providing a range of simple definitions and giving the lay of the land we will be exploring in this book. Key amongst this is that in performing your role as a manager you will be exposed to a set of sometimes conflicting pressures: representing the needs of the organisation in pursuing a change, the interests of your team and team members, your personal requirements. On top of this, you cannot forget the challenge of keeping a team operating and doing your normal daily work while changing.

Key concepts to take forward to the next chapters in this book are the concepts of different interests, resistance to change and sustaining change.

In pursuing change you will gain by both thinking about the short-term goal of delivering the change required, and the longer-term aim of developing your skills that will establish you as a credible change leader.

You are now ready to take the first steps on your journey.

CHAPTER 2

Start from the right place

A journey will be easier or harder depending on where you start from. The same is true of change. Some environments help change, some hinder change. In this chapter I want to share some ideas of activities you should focus on so you commence every change from the best starting point by creating an environment which helps rather than hinders change. You want your team to begin each change nimbly in their best running shoes, not in lead boots and tied down with large bundles of old luggage.

Many of the topics discussed in this chapter are simply good management disciplines – such as doing the HR basics of creating relevant job descriptions and having up-to-date performance appraisals. In the context of change, these disciplines become not only good practice, but key determinants of success. In fact, some of these disciplines only become truly valuable when you start delivering change. As a result, sometimes when change is not prevalent these disciplines become less focussed on and deprioritised as 'boring admin' or 'pointless bureaucracy'. In reality, they are the foundations for smooth change.

You will not know in advance all the changes you will need to undertake with your team, but you can be certain you will undertake some change. There is real value in executing these disciplines, and doing them right. These foundations will also help in developing your resilience and your self-sufficiency in delivering change in your team.

Understanding your team, its role and how it works

It seems rather too apparent that to change something you need to know what that thing is. Therefore you obviously need to know what your team does before you are going to change it. Yet I am regularly faced with managers who when pushed have to admit they don't really know what all their team members do on a daily basis. I don't mean to imply you need to know what every member of your team is doing every second. Nor do I mean you have to be an in-depth expert in all the areas your team are experts in. I do mean that you have to have a broad-brush understanding of what your team members can do, are doing and how they do it.

The starting line for successful change is to have some basic information about your team. What do your team members *actually do* on a day-to-day basis (as opposed to what you may think they are meant to be doing, or what their job definitions say they do)? Why do they do these things? Are they doing the right things?

There is a stream of simple questions you can ask yourself to find out how well you understand your team, its role and how well it works. Let's look at some more of these questions.

Who are your key suppliers? By which I mean: what inputs from where does your team take to do its work? Are those inputs of the quality your team needs? At the other end of your work, who are your key customers? Who takes whatever you produce and are they happy with it?

What are your team's main tools, processes or procedures? Are they the best or can they be improved? Where do these processes fit within your organisation's wider business processes? Is the work of your team core to the success of these business processes or do you perform a peripheral role? If you look at the organisation from an end-to-end process perspective, what are the potential threats and opportunities facing your team?

If you look beyond your organisation's boundaries to the wider economic, competitive and technological drivers, are there any other potential threats or opportunities facing your team?

Is your team doing a good job – and how do you know? Is this just a personal judgement or do you have an effective set of performance metrics and a reliable set of data to show how your team perform against these metrics?

I hope you can answer questions like these. If you can't, then you need to do some homework. Trying to pursue change when you cannot answer simple questions like these is liable to end up with unnecessary problems as your assumptions and lack of knowledge exposes you and your team to risk.

In asking these questions I am not trying to suggest you need to do an exhaustive and detailed analysis of the daily work of every team member. But you do need a practical, current, working knowledge of the team and the context in which the team exists.

> you do need a practical, current, working knowledge of the team and the context in which the team exists

As an aside, you probably need that knowledge to manage the team effectively in the first place, irrespective of change.

I want to add one more question: what is your vision for the team? Ideally, you have a vision for your team. When you know what your team does today and how it does it, how does that compare to your vision for the future? Not all team leaders have a vision for their team, but it is useful to have one. The advantage of having a clear vision is that it makes it more likely that you will be the originator and driver of change as opposed to responding to changes imposed on you. (This is explored more in chapter 3.)

The management and HR basics

In most organisations there is a range of management and HR basics which are built into the way the organisation operates. Two critical parts are job descriptions and regular documented performance appraisals. Almost everyone dislikes the task of developing these. Doing so can seem like the worst of a big organisation's red tape. They seem a million miles from acting as the innovative, creative and flexible employee the world of work seems to need nowadays. In reality, these basics come to life in many change situations. How easy or hard your change will prove to be will frequently depend on how well you have put these fundamentals in place.

Job descriptions only have value if they are documented and are relevant to the roles people actually perform today (and not five years ago when they were last updated). You do not want to create overly rigid job descriptions as this can create a barrier to flexibility. But you do need something that is a reasonable reflection of the role and expectations of the role of each of your team members.

Performance management processes typically result in some form of annual appraisal. Managers can become very lazy with regard to appraisals – treating them as a tick-box exercise where the goal is to maximise team members' satisfaction and not carry out the spirit of the process. I regularly come across teams in which everyone has been graded high performance or all the reviews are out of date.

Doing annual appraisals can often seem like a dull and unimportant bit of paperwork, especially if your budget for pay rises and bonuses makes no real effective difference to anyone. However, when it comes to change, having done meaningful performance appraisals can make your life significantly easier.

Many changes require alterations to job roles. If you do not have a history of meaningful job descriptions this can be harder to achieve than necessary. It is even worse with redundancy. Some changes unfortunately require a selection process which will result in people being made redundant. If everyone in a team is being made redundant then the process, while painful, is relatively straightforward. However, once you have to do any form of selective redundancy then a past history of meaningful performance appraisals will help you tremendously. If you have no appraisals that really differentiate between people's performance then the grounds for selection can be dubious.

This is not just about workload. If you do not have the right job descriptions or have not done proper performance appraisals you risk being perceived as being biased or unfair in the way you make decisions regarding your team and the changes. Worse than being unfair, you may be breaking employment law. You need specialist advice in this area, but generally you should appreciate that it is easy to find yourself being accused of discrimination, constructive dismissal or unfair dismissal. The point in overcoming such accusations is not whether you can verbally and honestly argue that you have not been unfair, but whether you can prove it by pointing to historic documents such as job descriptions and performance appraisals.

Whatever your views of the merits of job descriptions and performance appraisals, without them you risk finding yourself quickly in difficult waters when it comes to certain common types of change. Additionally, your workload, when any change arises which affects the shape of people's jobs, can increase significantly. On the other hand, adherence to basic HR policies will make your life significantly easier and many of your changes less risky and quicker.

In some organisations I have worked with, when I start to ask about job descriptions and performance appraisals I can sense I am being regarded as a combination of dinosaur and killjoy. Perhaps those organisations never change. Such an attitude often reflects naivety and a lack of experience of how painful change can be. No one starts a business or a management career with the thought of making people redundant. I hope you never have to make anyone redundant and perhaps you will be lucky. But if you expect to employ people or work as a manager for many years, it is likely that sooner or later you will. If you do, then getting these basics right is key to a smooth process, which is better for everyone involved.

Relationships with the team

Resilient and successful teams are built from strong relationships. There is a level of trust between the individuals in the team. The individuals in the team understand each other's roles, strengths and weaknesses. When there are problems people will tend to naturally work together to find solutions.

great leadership is built on relationships

The benefits of strong relationships stretch to the team's line manager. A team who believes and trusts their manager is obviously in a better position than one that does not. A team that wants to follow their manager as a leader is often presented as the best situation for organisational teams. Great leadership is built on relationships.

Trust between a manager and the team will be useful in change as a manager seeks to steer the team along the best path to the end point. A team that trusts its manager and believes in her vision will respond to change more positively than one that does not.

Trust can be both enhanced and damaged by change. Organisational interests will conflict with team members' interests from time to time. Sometimes you will have access to information you cannot share with your team. Situations in which you know something your team is not yet aware of, and when they do become aware of it they will regard it as detrimental, will test your personal strength – and at times your ethical position.

One point is worth clarifying: a strong relationship is not the same thing as a personal friendship. For me, personal friendships are one of the most important things in life. However, personal friendships between team leaders and their team members can be mixed blessings. A strong friendship can be the basis of a productive partnership between team leaders and team members. Yet unless friendships are uniform across the team, which is unlikely, individual friendships can lead to perceptions of bias.

How you respond to friendships depends on your style and personal traits. Some people find it hard to give an honest performance appraisal, especially a critical one, to a close friend. If you struggle with this, you may also struggle with driving a change programme with a group of friends who are resistant to the change – especially when that change is perceived as being opposed to their interests.

When it comes to friendships the best answer is to be natural and know yourself. Friendships have a habit of just arising with or without planning – but you do have some control. If you have the ability to be both truly friendly and to do effectively what your job as a team leader requires, then go ahead and make friends with the team. If not, then be a little careful and keep some emotional distance from team members. That does not mean you have to be cold and aloof – you should be able to interact in a friendly style without being friends.

Relationships outside the team

There is a range of relationships every manager should seek to develop. You need a relationship with your boss, your customers and your suppliers. There is usually a wider group of stakeholders who can influence the success and perception of your team. Developing relationships with these people is advantageous for a number of reasons. On top of this, a broad network of relationships with your peers will help.

Such relationships are always helpful for the smooth operation of your team and for your own career development. But their usefulness increases in situations of change. For example, if you have a wide range of strong relationships, you:

- Have people on whom you can call for help and advice when things do not go so well. This is always a real risk during change.
- Will be able to set expectations, and customers will tend to have greater patience when your operational performance dips as you implement change (see chapter 6).
- Have access to a wider set of eyes and ears for what else is going on in your organisation which may affect or influence the change.
- Can share and test ideas and opportunities for improvements, and discuss where you should prioritise your efforts.
- Gain additional resources when you are struggling with your work through the change cycle.

I have already spoken about self-sufficiency as a manager. The truth is, to misquote a famous phrase, *no manager is an island.* It may seem that a better and stronger network of relationships around your organisation makes you less self-sufficient. In reality, the better your network the more independent you can be as it means you will be less dependent on any one individual relationship or viewpoint. This increases resilience.

You will, of course, develop relationships as part of your normal day-to-day work. Don't rely on passively acquiring the relationships you need. I believe relationships are fundamental to the effective working of your team, and your ability to guide the team through change when it occurs. You should actively identify the people you would benefit by having relationships with and seek ways to develop those relationships. There is plenty of evidence that more successful managers tend to have larger networks of relationships at work, and actively work to expand and improve their network.

Expectations, entitlements and contracts

Expectations and entitlements

As a manager you want to have a good relationship with your team. You want to reward team members for their hard work and successes. You want to make work enjoyable and fun. Let's imagine a common scenario. Your team does some brilliant work. You do something in response – you arrange something simple like a party, you give a small gift, or you just let someone go home early. Fortunately, you work in a good team, and so you start doing this often. After a while you forget the reason why you do this and it becomes a habit. The team now expects it. Unfortunately, the team now regards it as an entitlement.

This may seem a pessimistic scenario. But ask yourself: are there any non-binding but widely accepted entitlements in your team? You might be surprised by the things which you clearly think of as discretionary which can be stopped at any time, but which your team have come to regard as part of the basic benefits of working for the organisation. Such expectations of entitlements can often be a barrier to change and a source of tension during change.

I have often been involved in changes which have a significant impact on individuals, whether this is as simple as changing office location or as complicated as redundancy. Not surprisingly, people often resent these changes, but the truth is that in the vast majority of cases people accept a good rational argument for why a change is being pursued and make the best of what is a difficult situation. The irony is that this is not true for many smaller things which seem as if they should not matter much, but in practice they do. Small entitlements are a good case in point. The funny thing about many entitlements that people develop strong emotions about is how trivial they really are.

Let's look at some expectations and entitlements that can cause endless debate and stress in an organisation. The first is one that causes lots of arguments: job titles. Many people get very bothered by job titles. Personally, I regard job titles as pretty meaningless nowadays. I never make any judgement about someone when they tell me their job title because they are relative to context. In some organisations a Director or a VP is senior – in others these job titles can be given to quite junior roles. I can think of two of my clients with contrasting hierarchies. In one Directors work for VPs, in the other the opposite is true. It's easy to conclude therefore that job titles are trinkets that can be altered easily. But tread warily when you change job titles, a lot of people's personal esteem is related to their job titles. For many people a job title is not an optional marking of someone's role in an organisation, it is a badge of honour and success.

The sense of entitlement can stretch to what can often seem like bizarrely trivial things to get upset about. I have seen alterations in desk location, parking space locations, regular Friday afternoon drinks, Christmas parties and gifts of Thanksgiving turkeys causing serious and lasting resentment. You will find people making statements such as 'it all went downhill when we stopped the Christmas party' or 'when we stopped giving biscuits in meetings' (yes, really biscuits!) – even though that was several years ago. Depending on the culture there may be a whole list of other minor events, gifts and benefits which may be a potential source of tension if they are ever removed or modified.

The reduction of entitlements can sour relationships, resulting in loss of productivity and good will. In extremis it can result in labour disputes.

What is the answer? There is no perfect answer I'm afraid. Assuming that some things may need to be stopped someday, you might avoid doing anything which can ever be perceived as an additional benefit. That is too draconian and unnecessary. It is fair and encouraging to acknowledge people's efforts in terms of rewards and simple small gestures of thanks. Work should be pleasurable and these small events and gifts help to make it fun. They are also important parts of team motivation and developing your relationship with the team.

I have a few tips to help you navigate your way through this problem:

1 If it is something you do for your whole team try to make clear it is not an additional benefit, but just your way of saying thanks and you won't always do it in future.

2 When possible associate parties and events with specific achievements so it is not a general entitlement, but a specific reward for an identified result. This may mean only offering it to individuals or part of your team.

3 Make sure such rewards or events are timely, so they clearly relate to why they have been given. This also makes them impactful.

4 Be flexible. Keep changing the style of reward. Entitlements come about from a sense of expectation and habit. Anything that may be associated with the phrase 'we always do that' risks becoming an entitlement and risks being a problem when you need to change it. Variation is fun and it also reduces the risk of developing a sense of entitlement.

5 If you are thinking of removing an 'entitlement', make

sure the benefit is really worth the bad feeling it creates. Rarely will removing biscuits from meeting rooms save an organisation any significant money!

Rights and contracts

Of course, beyond entitlements there are the real rights that your staff have. Rights that are enshrined in law and regulations, or within their employment contracts. When you undertake any form of change, if you are concerned about impinging on any of these rights, seek advice. A good place to start is your HR department.

Many change initiatives have no impact on contractual terms and need to make no reference to contracts. Some of the more difficult changes do. In those situations, you are obliged to have an understanding of what is in your team members' contracts. If you were not the original recruiting manager, but have inherited a team – for example through your recent recruitment or promotion – you may be surprised as to exactly what is in some of those contracts.

There is one situation specifically worth looking out for when it comes to contracts. This situation arises when a company has grown over a long period of time, especially when it has developed through mergers and acquisitions. Often you then find that different members of your team have different contracts with differing levels of rights and benefits. Such differences can cause many difficulties during significant change initiatives.

A similarly complex situation can arise when you have a team geographically spread across countries and subject to varying legal frameworks, employment terms and cultural norms. For instance, notice periods can vary significantly. In some countries people tend to work their notice, in others they go on 'gardening leave', or depart immediately with their notice paid off.

You cannot avoid these problems, but you can certainly avoid making them worse by being familiar with what conditions and protections are in your team members' contracts. If you ever have to implement change which has a significant impact on roles, employment status or benefits, start with an audit of contractual terms. Seemingly benign differences, like different types of pensions, can cause huge variations in how you will need to handle individuals in the change process.

Competency and capacity

Identifying change opportunities, generating ideas for changes, working out how to achieve the change, delivering and sustaining change can create specific needs within your team. First, there is a skill or competency need. Do you or your team have the competencies to undertake a specific type of change you require? Secondly, there is a capacity need. Do you or your team have the capacity to perform the work required to deliver the change on top of your normal work?

Competency

Change may call upon a wide variety of skills and it is unlikely you will have the resources to be able to train a sufficient number of people in your team in every change skill that you might ever require. Some organisations focus on specific skills and approaches for change. For instance, many organisations have a trained cadre of six sigma or lean experts to help drive performance improvements and to embed a level of skill in every team in the organisation.

Let's assume you accept that change is part of the regular rhythm of your organisation. Then you should consider, as part of your normal process of capability and competency development for your team, what change management expertise or change-related expertise your team needs in future. Whether this is developed through change management training, or more specific skills development, like process design or root cause analysis, depends on your specific needs, your management approach, as well as the wider organisational approach to change.

If budgets and time for training are constrained then look to other ways to develop skills in the team. Let team members volunteer for company change projects so they can develop skills on the job. Get team members together to discuss change experiences – sharing their knowledge across the team. Ask someone to read a book on change and précis key relevant ideas for the team. Developing skills does not need to be a significant resource drain.

Capacity

Change is an ongoing part of most organisations and therefore you should also consider what capacity you need in your head-count or budgets to perform change. If you are a very small team with a handful of people it is likely you will just have to 'find the resources' within your existing capacity. Then resolving the challenge may come down to the timing and prioritisation of work. On the other hand, if you run a large team with dozens or hundreds of staff, you may be able to allocate some dedicated resources for change.

The need for change resources is specific to the individual context your team works in. It requires prioritisation relative to the other resources you need in your team, taking account of your budget and headcount constraints. It also depends on whether your organisation has any shared resources you can access, such as project managers, change managers and so on, when you want to undertake a specific change. Many organisations rely on contractors and consultants when it comes to change, but that means you may never build up the skills in-house. Whatever is the right answer for you, when you are doing your resource planning you should at least consider how you will build change skills into the mix of team skills for when you will need them.

Dealing with gaps

In this chapter I have outlined a number of different aspects you can consider as your starting points for change. When you undertake any change will it be an uphill battle from day one – or do you have a strong basis to move forward from?

You have certain levers which are applicable to change as well as general management tools. You may or may not have developed these in the past. If you have not, then you may be at a disadvantage when it comes to your change initiatives. It is often during change when all the standard good day-to-day line management practice pays off.

What if you do not have all of these fundamental aspects discussed in this chapter in place? First, don't panic. Rarely is anyone perfect in all these areas. It takes time to get a team to a position of maturity in which all the things which are regarded as normal line management are actually done. The fact that you are not doing all of them will make you no different from many other teams.

While this should give you comfort, it is not an excuse for doing nothing about it! To approach filling the gaps:

● Start with the management basics – job descriptions and performance appraisals. If you are behind on these then today is as good a day as any to start working on them.

● For some of these aspects one answer may actually be to run a small project, for example a short project to assess and clarify your skills and working processes.

- In doing your longer-term planning and budgeting think about building in-team training, skills development and building the capacity you need for change.

- Where you think you have a gap that will expose you and the organisation to risk in future changes start building the case for additional resources in time for the next budget round. Your boss will receive lots of requests for additional resources every time budgets are set. You will not always win these arguments, but you will never get anything if you do not ask for it!

Filling the gaps will not happen overnight, but you can regard it as part of the normal continuous improvement of your team and building your team's resilience. This will help you – but not just you. It will enable your team to make a fuller contribution to future organisational change programmes. Developing change-related skills will help team members individually in their future careers.

brilliant recap

In this chapter we have discussed some of the fundamental aspects of everyday line management which can help or hinder your change. The main lesson is that what you do when the team is not changing will affect how quickly and smoothly you can guide the team through change when it does occur.

Reflect on your team and consider:

- If your understanding of your team, its role and how it works is strong enough to identify and guide the right change.
- Whether the management and HR basics, especially job descriptions and documented performance appraisals are in place and up-to-date.
- The relationships you have within the team and across the organisation and how these help or hinder you with change.
- What expectations and entitlements team members have and how you avoid building any further sense of entitlement that can constrain change.
- What is in your team members' contracts and the implications for change.
- The capacity and competency your team has to undertake change.

It is unlikely that you will be perfect in all these areas. No one ever is. Build activities into your continuous improvement and team development to fill any gaps. Don't let this just happen in an unstructured and ad hoc manner – drive it proactively as part of developing a stronger, resilient and more productive team for future challenges.

CHAPTER 3

Finding clarity, making clarity

f you seek advice or read a book on implementing change, running projects or making improvements in your team you will soon be encouraged to identify and explain your objectives or goals for the initiative. If you enter a conversation about the future of your team, for example in your annual appraisal with your boss or at a team meeting, you will find yourself being asked to clarify your *vision* or *strategy* for the team. These are related questions. All of them are ways of asking: where are you going, which direction are you taking the team?

Strategies and visions have a close relationship with change. There is a whole lexicon of related concepts, which are part of management language but which we do not need to explore here in any detail. Different organisations use different terminology: strategies, aims, missions, priorities, goals, objectives, outcomes or plans. The different words have various meanings, but are used often as partial synonyms and overlapping concepts. Essentially, they bring together two main strands of thinking at a high level: firstly, what the organisation wants to achieve, and secondly the main pillars of achieving this. When it comes to an individual team we can ignore much of this complexity, and for simplicity's sake in this chapter I am going to stick mainly with the term vision, as in 'the vision for your team'.

Change is often a result of an innovative vision, and experience shows that change is best tackled when there is a clear vision of where you want to go. For me, a vision is simply a shared image of how you want your team to be and which direction you want to lead the team to get there. In this chapter I will describe the need for, challenges and approach to developing a clear vision for the team.

The classical myth

There is a simple classical model of how organisations work. Someone at a senior level – probably the chief executive – defines *the* strategy. This describes a grand vision of the organisation of the future and how to get there. This strategy is communicated, or cascaded down the organisation to each team. Each team applies the strategy to its area of responsibility. As all the teams implement the strategy in their areas of responsibility, the strategy gets rolled out across the whole organisation. If the chief executive has defined the right strategy, the organisation will gallop off into the sunset enjoying huge success.

Anyone who has worked in any organisation for any length of time knows that this model is not only a simplification, it is largely a myth. There are lots of reasons why organisations do not work quite like this in practice.

There is rarely *a* clear strategy. There may be simultaneously several different strategies or bits of strategy coming from different levels in the management hierarchy. The strategies may be altered unintentionally as they are cascaded down an organisation, like a giant game of Chinese whispers, until what reaches the team at the bottom of the hierarchy bears, at best, a partial resemblance to what was discussed at the top. Translation or interpretation of broad global strategies to local team contexts is often imperfect. On top of this, strategies may not relate to the work of everyone in an organisation. Those who sit outside the scope of the strategic vision may try to adapt it to their work or create their own vision with more or less success. Some people may deliberately ignore or miscommunicate a strategy that they do not believe in or that is not in their interest. Finally, it takes time to communicate a strategy across a complex organisation – and during that time the needs of the organisation may change, leading to a constantly adapting strategy. Keeping the whole organisation aligned with the most current thinking can be challenging. One way of bringing all these points together is to say that an organisation is full of friction and the flow of ideas and instructions from the executive level across the organisation is awkward, slow and subject to energy loss.

These are all reasons why top-down strategy is imperfect. Another reason is that strategy does not just go top-down. People at all levels in an organisation have innovative ideas, passions and beliefs, and have their own visions for

> people at all levels in an organisation have innovative ideas, passions and beliefs

the future. Not everyone is able to express, promote or influence others with these visions, but usually a sufficient number of people are and they act as alternative sources of vision. Strategic ideas can come from the bottom up and across peers in an organisation. Most organisations actively encourage and benefit from innovative ideas being generated at all levels of the organisation.

Another issue is that definitions and expectations of strategy vary immensely. If you don't believe me tell 10 people sitting in a room that you are going to deliver a strategy for them. Then ask them to write down on a piece of paper, without conferring, what they expect to receive from you. I doubt you will get 10 equivalent sets of words. They will be significantly different. The truth is that there is limited consensus as to what a strategy is, what its tangible manifestation is and what it is for. I don't doubt you can find a definition of 'strategy' and get some consensus around this definition. I am saying that in most organisations this consensus does not exist across the board – and yet virtually everyone uses the term *strategy*. Ironically, there is usually a unity in a specific sentiment about strategy. It is a yearning for greater clarity: 'if only there was a strategy' or 'if only the strategy was clear'. Precisely what that thing called strategy would have to be like to be clear is vague!

Unless something is done about this, there is a danger of a meaningless cacophony of noise coming into your team rather than a coherent strategy. It is part of your job as a team leader to deal with and sort out this noise of contending voices. Rarely as a team leader will you simply be handed a clear and unambiguous set of instructions. Most of the time you will have to set out to find clarity and sometimes you will have to make clarity for yourself. The absence of a clear strategy being handed to you on a plate is no reason for complaint – it is one of the reasons team's require managers! Looked at positively, it gives you freedom to decide what is best for your team.

If you want your team to be effective they need to understand their role, understand their boundaries and ideally understand the vision for the team. If this vision requires change, then those changes need to be prioritised relative to each other and relative to the other work the team needs to do. *This is finding and making clarity.* I believe that the activities of finding and making clarity for a team are some of the most important for a team leader.

the activities of finding and making clarity for a team are some of the most important

If you spend your time waiting for the perfectly clear vision for your team to be given to you, you will wait a long time. As you wait, you risk your team and its role becoming out-dated and irrelevant. But a vision for your team cannot be generated from nowhere. There are the ever-present pressures for change to be considered. At its simplest, you will find yourself dealing with three types of impetus to change:

1 ***External goals and target setting:*** most often you
   will have some top-down mandates handed down to you
   by your boss to implement. These will not be defined in
   terms of specific tasks for your team to do, but in terms
   of prioritised targets such as improving margins, reducing
   costs, increasing staff satisfaction or keeping within a
   percentage tolerance of your budgeted headcount levels.
   The more senior you get the more often you will be
   presented with targets to achieve rather than specific actions
   to perform. In this situation you need to determine how
   to achieve this target, and then make it meaningful and
   applicable to your team.

2 ***Externally imposed actions:*** however, from time to time,
   your team will be given a very clear set of instructions and
   be told what to do. Your boss may just mandate that you
   need to do X. There may be an explanation of why you
   need to do it, but sometimes there will not. The request or
   instruction may be part of a wider change initiative going
   on across the organisation. As a team leader you need to
   assess X, and break it down into meaningful and achievable
   actions for team members.

3 ***Internal innovation:*** on top of external imposed ideas,
   you and your team will have your own creative insights. You
   know your work best and your team is usually best placed to
   identify ways of making it better. If you and your team like
   to control your own destiny, the ideal situation is where the
   majority of changes are being identified by the team.

Each of points 1, 2 and 3 requires a slightly different approach
– but in each case whatever it is that you need or want to do has
to be assessed, clarified and integrated within the wider work of
your team. Of course, as well as doing 1, 2 and 3 you must do
the daily work your team exists to do. How you balance doing
1, 2 and 3 with your day-to-day work is the subject of chapter 6.

Why is clarity of vision so important?

Everyone understands the benefits of clarity – but is it really important enough to dedicate a chapter in this book to it? Yes, definitely, as it is an area many managers struggle with. Change can create confusion and brings risk to the smooth operation of your team. An effective team works together towards common goals, but there is a risk during change that people start to move off in different directions. They may not be in conflict, but they may no longer be pulling in the same direction. Often during change you want your team to be creative to suggest ideas and take ownership for improvements. This is difficult to do if there is no framework of the areas you want ideas in. The ideal vision reduces the risk of these problems, but at the same time provides sufficient leeway to allow your team members to respond flexibly. The risks can be mitigated with a clear, shared vision for the team.

With a vision you are aiming to help your team have a sense of their position in the organisation and from that to find a path to some better level of performance, to overcome existing problems or to better leverage their strengths and opportunities. A vision ideally outlines a better place that all the team members want to achieve. Such visions enable teams to:

- Create shared goals;
- Set boundaries and give focus to everyday thinking and creativity;
- Provide a common language to talk about the team and its future;
- Communicate direction in a meaningful way between team members;
- Provide a way to explain, position and value the team's daily work;
- Develop rationale and justifications for one approach to change over others;

- Prioritise between change options by focussing on those most relevant to achieving the vision;
- Provide the basis for planning, preparing and helping the team through change;
- Understand what is expected by your team, what can be expected to be done for your team, and what help you should get with your change;
- Justify the cost or risk of changes, and support buy-in and approvals.

Another way of looking at this is to ask what is the alternative to giving your team a clear vision? At one extreme you can give your team no guidance. Then you are abdicating your responsibility as a manager and risking chaos. The level of guidance required depends on the maturity and context of your team and its work. Whatever level is appropriate, some level of guidance is needed. At the other extreme, you could tell your team what to do in detail, step by step. Some managers do try to do this. I would recommend you don't for a host of reasons. Some of the most important reasons are that it is inefficient, it will exhaust you, it is highly demotivating for skilled staff, you miss all the great insights and ideas your team has, and it will lead to your staff lacking interest or buy-in to the end result of much of the work.

Experience shows time and again that people are most motivated and productive when they have a level of freedom around how to do their work. But there needs to be some way of avoiding chaos and ensuring your team are doing the right things.

As much as possible engage rather than instruct your team. By taking a middle line and providing a clear vision you give a framework or space in which your team can constructively work, while having the freedom to creatively explore improvements and develop towards shared goals.

The elements of a team vision

What form should a vision take? Visions can be presented in different formats – as Word documents, PowerPoint presentations, or better still in a story that is shared by all the team members. This story explains the role of the team, accepts there is always room for improvement and opportunities to be grasped and provides a meaningful, but simple, image of what the team could be like in future.

A vision for a team should help to answer the following questions:

- How do we add value to the organisation?
- Where do we want to end up?
- Why can't we stay where we are? Why is there a need for change?
- What is the urgency for change? Why is there pressure to change now?
- What needs to change?
- What is the expected result – what are the benefits of achieving the vision?

The vision is not meant to be detailed or prescriptive about the changes required, how they are done or who does them. It provides the overall sense of direction for a team. This direction is relevant to the large changes the team undertakes, but it is also relevant to the day-to-day minor enhancements team members make.

Later in this book we consider how to use the vision to develop specific change initiatives and plans.

Understanding your boundaries

I now want to explore the way you should approach finding and making clarity for your team. I have used the phrases *finding clarity* and *making clarity* deliberately. You do not have complete freedom as a manager to do what you want; you must fit within the approach, culture, rules and structure of the organisation you are part of. You have to understand and interpret the guidance from your organisation and make it clear for your team – that is finding clarity. But this may have gaps or omissions of critical parts of a vision for your team. Rarely does anyone understand the opportunities and threats facing your team and your team's needs better than you and your team. Therefore, on top of finding clarity, you have to fill the gaps and make clarity for your team.

Finding clarity starts with an exploration of your boundaries. You are seeking to understand the givens that you must adhere to, and the areas you are free to decide for yourself. There

> finding clarity starts with an exploration of your boundaries

are different ways of doing this. Some of the boundaries will be explicit and easy to understand; others will be implicit and built into the culture and ethos of your organisation. If you are new to an organisation these can sometimes be hard to identify, but identify them you must. If you have been in an organisation for a long time these implicit rules and boundaries will most likely be obvious to you.

The simplest and main way to understand boundaries is through conversation or discussion with your own boss, members of your team and other key stakeholders such as suppliers and customers. The conversation is most productive with those people you have a constructive and open relationship with. Through discussion you are seeking to understand what you can and cannot change, what you must adhere to, what you must do, and what you have freedom to develop yourself. This is not a static picture, it evolves and so your understanding of the boundaries needs to be regularly refreshed.

You should be seeking to have a current perspective of the answers to questions like:

- What direction or strategy is mandated for the team to follow?
- What are the givens for your team?
- What is expected of your team?
- What are the common assumptions of the organisation that you need to be aware of?
- What level of freedom to interpret or create do you have?
- What level of authority do you have – and what things do you need approval to change?
- What is important in the organisation? What are the values that are espoused – and what are the values that are actually observed in behaviour?
- What are the key performance metrics used in the organisation? Is the activity of your team aligned to this metric or not? How should your team's work contribute towards achieving what is regarded as important in the organisation?

The degree of freedom you have will vary from organisation to organisation and depends on your role and level of seniority. In some organisations you will have very limited freedom to shape your team's vision as something unique. You may be instructed simply to follow wider company guidance. But generally you not only can, but need to, fill in the gaps around what you find to produce a complete vision for your team. Typically the larger your team or the more senior your role, the more opportunity you will have to fundamentally shape your team's vision. But in some organisations a proactive and innovative junior team leader also may have significant discretion. Take what you can!

Once you know your boundaries you will understand the space you have to operate in. Generally, especially if you are relatively junior, it is best to try and work within your boundaries most of the time. But some of the most beneficial and radical changes are about breaking givens, boundaries and assumptions. For instance, in organisations switching from a functional to a process basis, or from a functional to a project-based organisation, team leaders will find the need to challenge many of these historic givens they have taken for granted. However, tread warily before doing this.

My point is not to avoid breaking boundaries completely, but simply that you cannot be challenging the givens of the organisation every day. When you do decide it is time to break some givens in an organisation you may need to prepare yourself for a hard battle. Sometimes that is required in change, and you should not back down from it when it is required.

With this in mind there are two major advantages of clearly understanding your boundaries and the givens of your organisation. If you know your givens you are unlikely to accidentally find yourself challenging them when you do not want or need to. On the other hand, when you need to challenge the givens it is much easier if they are things that are spoken about rather than hidden and unspoken assumptions. (An analogy can be made with the experience of dealing with many forms of bigotry – it is far easier to deal with explicit bigotry than to try and root out hidden and unspoken biases.)

Developing a clear vision

One way of developing a vision is for you as the team leader to take some time out from your normal work, to find some quiet space and to think about your team. As you think, you should consider all the challenges and the opportunities for your team and from this envisage a better place for your team to be. Your vision is then this image encapsulated in a way you can communicate to your team.

The actual manifestation of a vision can be very simple. You are running a team, not a vast organisation. The vision for a team should not be seen as an exercise in creating a textbook. It may be as simple as one sentence. But it is a very important sentence for you and your team. As important as the sentence itself is the way it is created and how it is applied.

A vision encapsulates why the team exists, what it does, where it is going and why it should go there. Like a good advert, given the context and history of the team, a vision may imply far more than the words actually say. Examples of visions are:

- To provide an excellent order processing service continuously reducing customer delivery timescales.
- To supply graphic design services at a lower price but equal quality to any external provider.
- To be *the* project managers of choice within the business.
- To provide a level of customer service that achieves a best-in-class benchmarked level of customer engagement.
- To be the finance function that is regarded as a true business partner and trusted advisor.

Who develops the vision?

Many visions have been developed by a team leader working alone. Some of them have been successful. As someone with extensive experience of change situations, I prefer for visions not to be developed by the brilliant insight of the sole leader, but by the whole team – as this encourages a sense of ownership for that vision and greater motivation towards achieving it. (If you have a very large team this may not be possible, but I'm sure you get the idea.)

One good way to achieve this is to set aside time for the team to spend together, ideally off-site or at least away from the normal interruptions of the office, email, instant messages and phones.

There, as a group, you explore your current position and where your team could get to. While the focus of a vision is the future, it is worth reviewing the past and why the team is how it currently is. By briefly exploring the history of the team it can be easier to show why a vision needs to be different, as the historic pressures and reasons that created the team in one way will have changed. Exploring history, combined with the simple question 'why' also helps in exposing assumptions.

The aim is to develop a shared vision through dialogue and debate. It can help if this meeting is facilitated by an independent third party. If you really want to maximise the benefit it can also be worth doing some research – how do similar teams to yours work elsewhere, and is there anything you can learn or adopt from them?

The reason I am so keen that the vision is developed as a group is that it helps with future changes. By being engaged in the process of developing the vision, it is much more likely that your team members will accept the vision and find it compelling. It becomes something shared and believed in. The vision is something valued. It gives meaning and direction to everyday work. Critically, the vision becomes something more than just the words. The words encapsulate a broader meaning for the team.

In later chapters we will look at the change process. All I will say now is that if your team already believes in the vision for the team, then one step in the process of getting acceptance for change is already complete. The team is prepared for change, and more likely to accept any specific changes that help in progressing the team towards the vision.

The characteristics of a good vision

Irrespective of how you manage the development of your team's vision you are looking for a specific sort of result. The result you want is a vision that is clear and meaningful to your team. The vision should be believable but challenging. The vision should be compelling and seen as worthwhile to achieve. The vision should be exciting to team members and start them pondering how to achieve it. Team members should associate with the vision. Finally, ideally the vision is consistent with and a logical extension of whatever organisational strategy is in place.

You can list many other criteria as positive assessments of a vision, but for me these are the most important.

Maintaining the vision

Visions need to be maintained, and should be regularly reviewed and refreshed. Periodically it is good to start again from scratch and develop a completely new vision – if for no other reason than if you have been successful you will have already achieved your previous vision. Your vision should indicate the journey you need to take. Once you arrive it is time for a new one. The skill is to keep enough stability so people do not feel they are constantly aiming at a moving target, while avoiding complacency in the team. An old vision can be like stale food – unappetising and unexciting. If your vision feels dull and does not create any excitement or urge to improve, it is time to revise it.

The speed at which a vision becomes yesterday's news is context specific. In some organisations a vision may be adding value for many years. In others with a faster pace of change, or less patience, visions may need to be updated more often. I suggest you revisit your team's vision at least once a year, even if you do not always end up modifying it.

Applying your vision

A great vision is not a sacred secret. It needs to be something that is shared and referred to by everyone in your team on a regular basis. It needs to be communicated again and again. It must be reinforced until it is a natural part of everyone in the team's thoughts and discussions. The way you assess team members' performance and give feedback should be relative to the change.

In this way the vision will form the backdrop to all of your daily work. It becomes a trigger for creating new ideas about what can be changed and how. A vision is not a panacea that will solve all your problems alone. But a shared vision will be a significant support in developing a unified and well-functioning team. It will also be a critical element in driving change.

> a shared vision will be a significant support in developing a unified and well-functioning team

There can be a risk that everyone takes the time to work on a vision, and then it is forgotten, like those old dusty documents on the top of our bookshelves. A vision is a tool for everyday use and it is only worth the effort of developing one if it makes a meaningful contribution to your team.

One way of thinking about developing a compelling vision for your tcam is that it is the first step on your team's change journey.

A special case: obsolete skills

We are living longer. We will all have to retire later. These facts mean we are all likely to work for longer. Factor into this the rate of social, economic and particularly technological change. This means most of us will have to learn new skills and forget old ones.

It's easy to recollect technologies that used to employ large numbers of people. Remember switchboards, typewriters, fax machines or pagers? Businesses like bookshops and music retailers seem to be in an inexorable decline. Skills like trans- lation are being automated. My first job was working on technology that is defunct, for a company that no longer exists, making a product which no one now buys. This is not unusual – and it is not just about the past. Technologies we currently regard as fundamental to work, and which many people base their jobs on, will become obsolete.

I do not know what the future will hold. I expect some people reading this book will have a skill set in short supply and in huge demand right now. You probably feel pretty confident about your employment prospects in the short run. But who knows what will happen with technology advance in the next 10, 20 or 30 years – a period in which you may still require employment. Even knowledge industries and the professions which have so far been relatively immune to employment changes may be threatened. With advances in robotics and artificial intelligence, what jobs won't be automated?

you are likely at some point to have to deal with teams with obsolete skills

I am not saying this to worry you, but to raise the real issue that as a manager you not only have to deal with exciting things like growing your team and improving your skills. You are likely at some point to have to deal with teams with obsolete skills. This is where a vision can become particularly useful – what is the role for your team in future, as the skills they have must change? Are you just going to accept obsolescence, or are you going to work with your team to build a vision for ongoing productive value to your organisation?

My personal experience, like many other people's, is one of continual renewal of skills. The best response is to be proactive and to look to upcoming threats to your team and decide on the best path to take. Putting your head in the sand is usually the worst approach. Whatever vision you have will dictate the shape, pace and scale of the changes required for your team – it may also determine whether the team members retain relevant skills or not.

A final thought: your role in strategy

Creating a vision for your team may seem like overkill. You may be thinking: but we are simply the team who performs function X. Surely all we need to know is that we are the team who does function X? We don't need all this vacuous thinking about strategy and vision. We just need to get on with our job.

I hope that only a tiny minority of readers at this point will be thinking this. There are many advantages to having a vision for the team. It gives a positive sense of belief to your team. It will help direct future changes. It may help you avoid obsolescence. And it does not need to be complex or radical.

There is another reason for developing a vision, which is a more personal reason for you. It relates to how you conceive of your role in your organisation. Do you see yourself as a victim of the organisation's strategy, an implementer of strategy or someone who has a voice that should be contributing to strategy? Do you see yourself in the final category? If so, there is much more chance of you developing this voice, and being perceived as someone with valid strategic input, if you have a clear vision for your team.

brilliant recap

The activities of finding and making clarity for a team are some of the most important for a team leader. By interpreting organisational strategy you can find clarity for your team. Often organisational strategy does not cover all the aspects required for your team – then you need to make your own clarity.

A shared compelling vision has many benefits for your team. It will help to identify, shape and prioritise the changes you undertake. If team members have been engaged in the development of the vision it will also ease the process of accepting changes.

To develop a vision, start by understanding your boundaries – what are the givens for you and your team and what freedom do you have to use your own creativity and ideas? Then develop your vision, ideally as a shared experience with your team. It should be regularly updated and revisited.

The vision must be continuously communicated and reinforced so it becomes the background to all conversations, planning and activity of the team.

CHAPTER 4

Identifying changes

I f you have a vision for your team and if you understand how your team operates now, you should be able to identify the gap between the two. The gap is what you need to bridge to achieve your vision. Driving change in your team is about identifying the best ways of bridging this gap and then implementing the selected changes in the most appropriate way. The logic of these points is clear and simple, but in reality, deciding what to do with regard to change can be difficult because there are so many things you could change and so many ways you could go about changing them.

In this chapter I describe the scope of changes available to you. I do this by considering the variable aspects in your team, which you can modify to drive the sorts of change you want to achieve. I then discuss different approaches to changing these variable aspects. This chapter cannot tell you what to change or not to change, but I can help you to build your own model of the different factors to consider in deciding what to change in your team. The aim is for you to start to build a prioritised change agenda for your team, which takes a balanced approach to the various options for improvement.

The identification of potential changes and approaches to implement those changes are the material of numerous management theories and fads. Ever since Taylor came up with his views of scientific management in the early 20th century there has been a stream of ideas concerning the best way to run organisations.

This chapter has been influenced by some of these, but I take a non-partisan view of management theories. I try not to get caught up in short-term theory fashions. I act like a magpie, picking the pieces I think are most useful. The theories come and go, each generation tending to bring some new ideas which influence the future generations of management thought. But underlying all of them is the constant search for new and improved ways of running organisations. That means change.

Are you originating or responding to change?

There will be many things you are told just to do and implement within your team. Your team operates as part of a larger organisation, and many of the most important and beneficial changes in the organisation will cut across many teams. Additionally, sometimes you will unintentionally be drawn into change initiatives going on elsewhere in the organisation. There may be changes in other teams, in tools or facilities such as IT systems, which although not originally considered or planned, have an impact on your team. Change a working practice in one team and it often has upstream or downstream effects on the workings of other teams. Modern organisations are highly complex, with many interdependent and interacting factors. It is rare that anyone really understands all of this end-to-end complexity and this means that often change in one area inadvertently has an impact in another area.

Organisations are subject to the law of unintended consequences – actions always have effects that are unanticipated or unintended. Effects on your team may be caused by changes that seem unrelated to your team. Rarely are these unintended effects purely beneficial. At times this will be annoying or frustrating for you and your team, but it is

actions always have effects that are unanticipated or unintended

just part of the reality of working in large organisations. There is little you as an individual manager can do about this apart from keeping your eyes and ears open to changes going on and raising the red flag if they affect you. Often, rightly or wrongly, you will end up having to adapt to these impacts.

The later chapters of this book are applicable whether you are the originator of change or merely responding to other changes, but the rest of this chapter focusses on the situation in which you and your team are the originators of change. Being able to identify and implement your own changes is important. You want to seize the opportunities you have to shape the future of the team. In reality, much of the change you implement will be as a response to wider changes in the organisation or directions from your own boss and other layers in the management hierarchy. Both can end up influencing or directly affecting your team.

The elements of team change

Let's start the discussion change originated by you by considering the variable aspects that go into making a fully functioning team within any organisation. I want to start by doing this to open your mind to the wide range of possibilities for change. I am using the phrase 'variable aspect' in a very broad sense as is shown by the list below (see Figure 4.1). I do not claim this list is exhaustive or that the items in it are fully mutually exclusive. Tweaks, modifications or complete redesign of any of these aspects can form the basis of team change. The list should give you a good flavour of the different possible features of your team you could consider changing:

- **The organisation of the team:** such as the number of team members, their arrangement into sub-teams, and their individual roles, responsibilities and interactions.
- **Ways of working:** how team members do their work,

which is usually encapsulated in processes, procedures and
work instructions.

● *Supporting tools:* what tools do the team use, or could
they use, to do their work effectively and efficiently.
This includes IT systems, manual tools and any other
instruments which support the team's work.

● *Facilities:* the facilities available to the team such as office
space, desk layouts, meeting rooms. Team performance
can be directly affected by the size, design and location of
facilities.

● *Skills:* the skills and capabilities of your team members.
What training or other forms of capability development are
used within your team and are there better ways? How do
you prioritise who gets what training?

● *Performance management and metrics:* the
performance management framework used, including
metrics and alignment with pay or other benefits. The
relationship between performance and performance
management approaches is often more complex than
assumed – but there is no doubt that team behaviour and
performance can be altered by modifying performance
management approaches.

● *Relationships:* what relationships do you and your team
have? Are these the right relationships to achieve your goals?
For example it is not unusual for organisations to want
to improve customer engagement. Even if your team is a
purely internally facing function, with no direct interactions
with real customers, you will have stakeholder relationships
that are important to you, and which may need to be
enhanced.

● *Culture:* for example seeking to adapt values and
behaviours. Cultural change can be one of the hardest
forms of change, and is likely to be significantly influenced
by wider organisational factors. Yet there are many examples

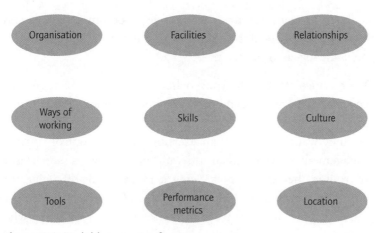

Figure 4.1 Variable aspects of a team

of managers who have successfully developed more productive or creative cultures within their teams. (It is also easy to find examples of managers who have inadvertently created negative and destructive cultures.)

● **_Location:_** team location and spread of locations can affect efficiency and cost. Is your team based in one location or is it geographically spread? Do you have to deal with multiple time zones and jurisdictions? Change may be related to consolidating locations, relocating or changing the basis of work, such as a shift towards home working.

Your leadership and management style

All of the points listed above are aspects of the way your team operates, and when you are thinking through change you should consider all of these. But don't stop there. On top of this one of the key aspects of change within a team is change to your style of management. One productive way of looking to achieve beneficial change in your team is to adapt your management and leadership styles. For instance, the way you delegate, give feedback to team members, your style of communication, and the way you do (or don't) act as a role model of the behaviour you want to see in the team.

Other critical factors in your behaviour can be considered as aspects of the management–leadership balance. How much space do you give your team members to do their work in the way they want to rather than exerting detailed control (micro-management)? How much do you operate as a supervisor controlling the team versus being a more hands-off delegator setting the direction in which they work? How much do you see yourself as the driver of work in the team versus someone who creates the space in which the team determines what to work on? There are many related considerations and there is no universal answer as to what is the right balance. However, experience shows that most teams thrive with greater freedom to do their work and less detailed interference from a manager, especially more senior and more experienced teams. Much of the debate over leadership versus management is concerned with this specific issue.

Whatever approach you take now is something you can choose to alter – and in altering it you will have a clear and often rapid effect on the team's levels of job satisfaction, motivation and performance.

Selecting aspects to change

In this section I have tried to give you the flavour of a catalogue of variable aspects you can modify in order to drive the change you want. It is important to understand that these variable aspects are not fully independent but are often overlapping and interacting factors. For instance, alterations to IT systems frequently require modifications to organisation, processes and training; or if you reorganise your team, you may want to align office layout and location to reflect that reorganisation. Making sure there is a coherence and systemic alignment between different variable aspects of your team is an important factor in successful change (we will look at this again in chapters 5 and 7; chapter 5 also contains a definition of the word 'systemic' for anyone unfamiliar with it – see Brilliant tip, 'What is systemic alignment?').

Approaches to change

Radical or evolutionary change?

Having started to think through which variable aspects of your team you would like to change, the next thing to consider is the approach to change. Are you looking for incremental improvements to what you already do, or do you want to pursue a sweeping transformation, where you rip up the rule-book and design some part of your organisation from scratch? The choice is essentially between the following two:

- **Radical change**, which can be quick, overcomes large problems and challenges well entrenched views and ways of working. But radical change can be risky, disruptive to your team and operational performance, and may require additional funding and resources.

- **Evolutionary change**, which can accumulate huge improvements over time and reduce the risk of disruption to the team and operational work, but by its very nature it has a slower pace. Evolutionary change tends to work with a particular mind-set and is unlikely to challenge the givens of your organisation. Occasionally, you need to revisit the fundamental boundaries, assumptions and givens of your team.

Some care is required in choosing how to achieve your goals. Radical and evolutionary change are often presented as competitors. They needn't be. You should expect over your career to be involved in both types of change, and often simultaneously. Generally it is appropriate to have an ongoing 'background' level of continuous change alongside occasional more fundamental changes.

The Total Quality Management approach, which people rarely talk about nowadays, was one of the forerunners of the continuous improvement movement. While it is largely forgotten, the idea of enabling team members to track performance, identify opportunities to improve and make ongoing adjustments to processes and tools has been successfully ingrained into many organisations' management practice. The aim is to achieve a state in which continuous improvement in itself is not regarded as change, but is simply thought of as part of the normal day-to-day activity of the team – that is continuous improvement as the business-as-usual style of work.

> the aim is to achieve a state in which continuous improvement in itself is not regarded as change

Fixing faults or building on strengths? Solving problems or seizing opportunities?

When discussions turn to improvements, most managers have been indoctrinated with the thinking of identifying problems and then resolving them. The prevailing management approach is to measure performance and to seek ways to improve that performance by identifying difficulties staff have doing their work. Associated with this thinking are techniques like root cause analysis, and the cycle of measure–analyse–improve. While the approach of continually identifying faults and improving on them has enabled many organisations to increase quality, productivity and other typical business goals, you should avoid the obsession of *only* finding faults.

To improve a team you do not only have the choice of trying to make fewer mistakes, you also have the choice of identifying a team's strengths and trying to leverage them more. Rather than worrying about doing less wrong, at least sometimes worry more about doing more right.

This is a counterintuitive way of thinking for many managers. I have regularly run workshops with teams working in a traditional problem-fixing mentality and when I ask them to list all their strengths and what they do best, they struggle because they are so used to thinking in terms of problem identification and resolution. Their lists of things they are good at start with things like 'identifying and fixing problems'. That is not the sort of thing I mean. Strengths in a team could include flexibility, creativity, unique insight and understanding into a customer's needs, multicultural and multiple languages, particular insights into a technology and how to utilise it, or a powerful set of stakeholder relationships. If your team has some strengths like this then why not think about how to leverage them more?

There is evidence that exploring and applying a team's strengths rather than continually searching for problems to fix has a number of advantages. Generally, it is easier and more natural for people to build on their strengths than to spend time trying to fix all their weaknesses. Think of brilliant sports players – they have become brilliant usually by focussing on an area of strength, not by continually trying to do something they do not have a talent in. Additionally, the continual focus on finding and fixing faults can create a negative atmosphere. It is usually a much more positive experience to focus on building on strengths.

Appreciative inquiry is a specific technique for focussing on strengths and envisaging positive futures for teams. If this is an area that interests you it is worth seeking out specific references or training in this area as it is beyond the scope of this book to go into it in any detail. One aspect of appreciative inquiry which is worth highlighting is the importance of the way people talk and frame questions about the future states. This has a significant impact on the type and quality of the outcomes achieved. The language you use as the team's leader is critical in this.

Focussing on the positives can also lead to an emphasis on change by leveraging opportunities rather than fixing problems – for example, taking advantage of some unused functionality within an ERP system to increase productivity or quality. There is nothing wrong with fixing problems, and it is likely as a manager you will spend a fair proportion of your time responding to issues and overseeing their resolution. But you will miss many of the most interesting, enjoyable and beneficial changes if your focus is solely on problem resolution.

Projects, targets or leadership behaviours?

Another way to think about how you approach change is whether you think of changing as an event outside of your normal work, or as a normal part of your day-to-day work. In the first case change can be undertaken as a project; in the second, change is part of your operational process. The typical way of driving this process is setting targets for the team and leaving them to decide how they will get on and achieve them. Another way of driving change is through behaviour – typically yours in the way you choose to lead the team. Your behaviours will influence the behaviour of the team, and by altering your behaviour you will influence changes in the behaviour of the team.

> your behaviours will influence the behaviour of the team

It is wrong to think of these as completely independent approaches. Project goals may be supported by changes to performance management systems and by your behaviour as the leader of the team. The issue is one of relative balance of effort as opposed to being mutually exclusive approaches to change.

Projects should be considered when the work to design and

implement a change has any of the following characteristics: complexity, requirements for skills outside those of your team, elements of risk or requires interactions between different team members or outside the team which need hands-on coordination. Other reasons to achieve change through projects relate to resources and budgets. If your endeavour requires an investment which you need to track in detail, then a project can be the ideal structure to do this. Additionally, if the work has complex interdependencies and timing factors to consider then utilise a project. Essentially, a project should be considered whenever there are issues of risk, coordination and/or complexity.

It is easy to find examples of changes which are best undertaken as projects – IT systems enhancements, the building of new facilities or new product developments. These are good exemplars of activities which are often best done as projects and not integrated into everyday work.

Projects have a resource overhead in terms of someone providing the management – that is, the project manager. (For larger programmes you can require a project management team.) Projects are best run by someone with an understanding of and experience in project management. The benefits of well-run projects have been proven time and again. The effectiveness of a team working with a project manager in terms of increased speed, reduced cost and reduced risk of delivery of change has been shown repeatedly. However, poorly designed or badly structured projects have also been shown regularly to waste resources. The lesson is simply that if you are going to run your changes as projects then do it properly. If your team is engaged in projects regularly it is worth investing in developing project management skills within your team.

On the other hand, many changes can be achieved through day-to-day activity and reinforcement. Reinforcement includes benefits and rewards resulting from your performance management approach, but also includes simple things such as the feedback you give as a manager to the team, what you praise and criticise, the topics you focus on when you talk and your daily management behaviour.

There is no simple model for which approach is best. Radical change often requires some form of project structure with a dedicated project team. Continuous and evolutionary improvement can normally be achieved as part of the day-to-day work of the team. A combination of the two can be most effective.

Proactive or reactive change?

Another consideration in relation to developing ideas for change is what stimulates your team to undertake change. For instance, consider the group who operates downstream from you in business process terms as your customer, whether they are an external or internal customer. Do you make improvements to satisfy your customers? If so, do you do what they ask for and wait for them to ask for it, or do you try to undertake innovative improvements that they have not yet thought of or discussed with you?

As an example of this, imagine you are responsible for the order management team. Let's assume this team operates downstream of sales, who generate the initial orders, and upstream of fulfilment, who actually fulfil the customer order (see Figure 4.2). If fulfilment are having problems with the way you pass orders to them, do you wait for them to complain or do you proactively seek improvements?

There is no easy answer to the question of how proactive you are in seeking improvements. To some extent it depends on the role and skills of your team. I always think it is worth on a periodic basis trying to identify upcoming opportunities to improve the service your team provides – and to consider any threats which may arise if you do not do this. Then you can decide whether

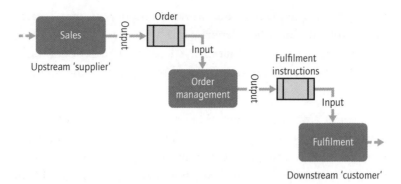

Figure 4.2 Example of upstream and downstream teams

the opportunity for change is potentially sufficiently beneficial to include it within the portfolio of changes you undertake.

The general mind-set of managers seems to be that it is better to be proactive than reactive. In many situations it is better to be proactive, to be ahead of the game, but it is too simplistic to think that you can always do this. You may not know of certain problems until a customer complains. Even if you do, you may not have the spare resources to prioritise effort on innovative thinking or investigation of creative possibilities. Additionally, there will be many changes, that, unless you are the largest of organisations with proper research departments, you probably cannot predict. Social, economic and technological changes happen all the time. Some of them will need a response from your team.

Change yourself or encourage others to change?

Sometimes some of your greatest problems are not in the way you do work, but in the way work is done elsewhere in the organisation. There may be little point investing significant effort in improving the work of your department because you are so constrained by the effects of work done by other teams. This can been shown when you trace business processes across an organisation. Frequently poor work in one department creates huge problems in other departments who work further along that process. In these situations it is often worth spending a proportion of your time as a manager trying to get other departments to change the way they work.

This is not always easy. Sometimes teams may simply not know about problems they are causing for you. Friendly guidance from you will be enough to get them to adopt their work in ways which are beneficial to you. But this scenario does not always play out. Teams may have limited incentives to help other teams if they create work for themselves making improvements while the benefits are accrued elsewhere. Teams can be busy with their own issues and have little or no capacity to help you out. For this to work people have to be willing to step back from parochial interests and look at wider company interests. Approaches such as business process re-engineering and lean encourage this viewpoint.

You can of course simply escalate up the management hierarchy to get support for changes in other teams. You will almost certainly need to do this, but you should do it with care if you want to maintain good working relationships across the organisation. No one likes the finger-pointing manager. Try to present it as a constructive suggestion for the benefit of the whole organisation rather than a personal complaint about another team.

If you decide that you want to get other teams to change, do not argue in an emotional way but try to develop a fact-based argument. Emotion often results from honest frustrations. Emotion can lead to a passion to change. Passion can be an important part of a powerful argument, but just expressing emotions is rarely a good way to win a management argument. Think through carefully: as a result of that other team's work what is the precise impact on your team? Try to quantify the impact if you can. Ideally quantify the benefit if they make improvements on your behalf. If you cannot quantify it, try and find some examples that will generate support for you. A few powerful, fact-based anecdotes can help your cause tremendously. (Perhaps we should not be influenced by anecdotes, but the truth is we are – and therefore you can use them to your team's advantage.) If your case is strong enough you could even position yourself as trying to help the other team gain investment for improvements.

Of course, if you expect this behaviour in other teams, you should be willing to do it yourself. Keep yourself open to challenge and requests from teams who work downstream of yours – either as your direct customer or as an indirect user of your outputs. Especially if you are creating issues for them which you can easily resolve.

> keep yourself open to challenge and requests from teams who work downstream of yours

Let me share an example of a successful campaign to get another department to change. Many years ago I ran an order processing team. One of our biggest challenges in efficient working was the quality of work we received from the sales department. Order forms were poorly completed: key information was missing and there were errors in facts like customer addresses. Often they were completed by hand illegibly. Details of the product and services ordered were incomplete. Specific customer requirements that were important to an individual customer were often forgotten.

Much of my effort in driving improvements in my team was actually spent lobbying for improvements in the way the sales team filled in orders. This took concerted effort over many months as historically the sales team saw completing orders in a quality way as pure administration which in their minds was, frankly, below them. My drive to get them to change was made possible by the detailed records we kept of the percentage of orders that were problematic, the volume of customer complaints this generated and the way this slowed down order processing – which in turn critically delayed cash coming into the company.

I won the argument in the end, but it took months of collecting data and engaging stakeholders before my case was accepted and action was taken. It proved to be well worth it both in terms of direct order throughput and speed, but also in terms of staff morale. While I got few thanks from the sales team, sometime later they had fully taken the changes on board and just saw producing quality orders as business-as-usual. I could live without the thanks given how much it improved the daily nature of work in my team.

Team focus or a good corporate citizen?

A final thought on your approach to change. How much of your effort will be focussed inwards at improving the team and the team's performance, and how much will be orientated towards the organisation as a whole? In other words, will you invest any of your effort into being a good corporate citizen?

The simplest way to do this is to volunteer your team members as a resource for the big organisation-wide projects. Such projects always need willing and skilled team members – even though your team may only be a marginal beneficiary. How much you do this is up to you. There can be a direct benefit to your team in being a visible supporter of these big cross-organisational programmes, and it can be good for your team members' skill and career development. I personally favour being a good corporate citizen. However, always remember that while you may get thanks for acting this way, this will be forgotten if as a result your team fails to meet its expected performance levels because of lack of resources to do your normal work.

Prioritisation and change capacity

The final aspect of your approach to change I want to consider in this chapter is prioritisation. With a creative mind, an open and willing team, an understanding of how well your team performs, and a view of the organisation's evolving needs, you will not find yourself short of changes you could undertake. If you are a change-conscious manager then the danger is not the risk that your team remains static in the face of evolving needs and increasing expectations, but that your team becomes overly committed to change.

I am a strong advocate of change. I often find myself working with people who significantly underestimate the volume of change they can successfully implement. As a result, much of my time is spent lobbying for change. But I also come across situations in which teams struggle to deliver all the change they initiate, and the pace of change is so great that the team struggles to accomplish its normal operational work. The typical situation is that an evangelistic and ambitious manager loads the team down with changes. The team feels unstable and lurches in and out of periods of chaos. Change can be exciting and beneficial, but too much change can be exhausting. We all need periods of calm and stability. Continuous revolution may sound interesting – but in reality few people can cope with it.

The answer to this is prioritisation. Change takes effort, resources and exposes your organisation to risk. It takes time for team members to adapt to change. The rewards for well-designed and well-executed change fully justify these costs and risks, but your resources are limited. You can think of all the changes you may want to undertake as your change agenda. The answer is to prioritise the change agenda you can undertake relative to the change capacity you have.

Conceptually there are two aspects to this change capacity. The first is simply the amount of time you can carve out from doing the normal work of the department to allocate to change initiatives. Do you have any level of discretionary resource to allocate to change? You should consider this when you build your resource plans and budgets. The second aspect is the capacity of your team members to absorb change. Change takes time for people to get accustomed to, and to adopt (we will discuss this more in chapter 7). If you want individuals in your team to reliably deliver their standard work there is only so much change you can expect them to cope with at any one time. And remember, on top of the change you have originated within the team, there will probably be a significant volume of change from the wider organisation which your team needs to respond and adapt to. Individuals' capabilities to absorb change vary significantly – it is both easy to underestimate how much change people can take on board and yet in contrast it is also easy to underestimate the scale of change you are already asking people to undertake.

You will only understand your capacity for change by experimenting and seeing the results. Unless you have a very sophisticated and large team, the prioritisation of change agenda against change capacity is likely to remain more art than science, relying on a fair degree of management judgement. As the manager of the team, it is part of your role to develop an understanding of teams' capacity for change, and to prioritise your changes relative to this capacity. This is not just about achieving change, but is also about understanding risk to business-as-usual performance.

teams that work in very volatile situations will develop greater resilience to change

Sometimes you will get this wrong, and find you have bitten off more than you can chew. Then you will have to slow down the pace of change. Occasionally, you will have to defend the team from changes being proposed by your boss or other senior managers if you think your team has exhausted its capacity to absorb more change. Experience develops resilience. Teams that work in very volatile situations with many changes going on all the time will develop greater resilience to change over time.

brilliant recap

Much of the change you will have to undertake as a team will not be improvements you have identified and driven within the team, but reflect your team's position as one variable aspect of the wider organisation. Many changes will be initiated outside your team, but you will have to respond or contribute to these changes.

Within the team there are various variable aspects you can alter, including the organisation of the team, ways of working, supporting tools, facilities, skills, performance management and team culture. Do not forget that one important driver of change that is completely within your own control is your own behaviour and style of management and leadership.

Once you have identified aspects of the team to look to for change, there are different approaches to deliver change. Radical change seeks to make step changes in performance, but can be risky and disruptive. Evolutionary change or continuous improvement reduces the risk of disruption, but tends to be slower. When considering change, do not become mesmerised by the problems your team has, but think about how to utilise the team's natural strengths more. As part of your role as a manager you will have to both lobby for change elsewhere in the organisation and occasionally try to defend your team from external changes.

Having identified the range of possible changes you can undertake, prioritise your change agenda relative to the change capacity in your team. You should be ambitious about how much change your team can undertake, but you should also be alert to signs of weariness and performance dips because of change.

CHAPTER 5

Plan the change

So far we have discussed getting the team in the right position to change. In chapter 2 we looked at creating the environment in which change can thrive. In chapter 3 we discussed building the overall vision for your team. In chapter 4 we considered how to identify the changes you might want to undertake. In this chapter our focus shifts from doing the groundwork to implementation. Chapters 6–9 deal with the heart of change management – implementing and sustaining change. But even starting implementation requires a little patience and thought. Before implementing any change there is a need to plan for that specific change – a plan that presents practical steps to achievable goals.

Planning is the point in the life of a change when you move from considering theory, and doing the intellectual and participative task of creating a shared vision, to thinking about real-world issues and taking account of the messy reality of the organisation. While planning is still at the thinking part of change management, it needs to be at the practical end of thinking.

Sometimes preparation and planning is a short and simple activity which uses a small amount of resource. On other occasions planning is a complex and resource-hungry activity in its own right. One challenge you will sometimes experience is the pressure to be seen to be active and making progress, while you really need to spend more time planning. Planning can seem like a low-value activity, the domain of the hesitant manager.

Organisations often favour the bold and dynamic. In truth, planning is often essential to reducing the risks associated with change.

The precise nature and extent of the planning work required is context specific, and in this chapter I focus on planning for a major and significant change within your team. To actually develop a plan for change you should also take account of the topics covered in the following chapters, as they outline in more detail the activities you should undertake in implementing change, which should form the content of your plan. You can also refer to the checklist shown at the end of Chapter 9.

Planning and plans

Not everyone is enamoured of planning. I regularly find myself working with teams that are undertaking change, that do not seem to have any sort of meaningful plan – and that resent the idea they should do more planning. Why do I think you should go through the sometimes time-consuming process of planning? The reasons derive from the fact that change can be complex and risky. Simple, low-risk changes – such as a minor modification to a procedure done by a single person – do not need detailed plans. But once you enter the realm of complex changes, requiring the involvement of multiple people and exposing your team to risk, you need to plan.

By planning you can find an effective approach to doing the work across your team rather than chaotic individual actions. By planning you can increase your efficiency, as you identify approaches to change which are relatively less intense in resource usage. By planning, you can identify the risks you may incur in undertaking change. Having identified risks you can do something to mitigate them. Planning makes you think through the balance between aspects of change such as risk, timing, resource usage, cost and so on. By planning you can reduce the risk of omissions. Change can be complex and it is easy to miss out tasks. Omissions will make your journey through the process of change harder. You can reduce the risk of omissions if you look at your team's change from a systemic perspective. Planning also provides the basis for estimating the resources and costs of undertaking a change. Budgeting will be essential for some changes.

A final point is the reason to plan: planning is ingrained into the expectations of most management hierarchies. If you need to gain approval and support for your changes, you will be asked to explain your plan. Whether or not you think this is worthwhile, plans also fulfil a political role as an expected part of management conversations about change. Like it or not, you will end up having to produce a plan.

Plans can be used in multiple ways. The most apparent is that they can help to structure your work. Plans can also support explaining what you intend to do to your team and other stakeholders. A plan can support you in managing expectations, for example by identifying when key events will happen in the change process and when you will be able to tell people key information about the change. This last point is useful, as often in change you will find an unfulfilled desire for communications when you have little or nothing tangible to communicate. The plan itself can help to fill this void, at least temporarily (see chapter 8).

However, a plan is not a cure-all for any problems that may happen during a change. A plan is a forward projection of what you think might happen. In reality, change is notoriously unpredictable and is unlikely to go exactly according to your plan. The only time a plan is absolutely correct is when the change initiative ends, and then the plan is merely an uninteresting historical record.

One possible response to the shortcomings of plans is to decide that you will not plan. This is the wrong response. Planning may not be perfect, but it is better to face a complex and risky task with a commonly understood approach than with no approach at all. The right method is to plan, but to accept that you will need to refine and adapt the plan as you go and the reality of the situation unfolds. We will return to this point in the next chapter.

The other point about plans is that there is no one right level of detail that is appropriate. The level of detail and effort you put into a plan should be decided pragmatically. What is the level of risk and complexity in the change you are about to undertake, and therefore what level of planning is justified? What is the level of knowledge you have about the change and the context you are about to execute it in, how volatile is the situation and therefore what level of planning is possible? In planning you should seek to balance these two points.

When people produce plans, they often focus solely on the work associated with the production of the plan as an artefact – a document everyone can refer to. This is important, but I believe that the process of planning is as important as the plan itself. I do not completely agree, but like the sentiment of the famous saying by Eisenhower: 'Plans are useless, but planning is everything'.

The planning process forces you to think about the activities in the change. If you create your plan as a team exercise, as I think is best practice, then the process of planning enables team members to develop a robust and shared understanding of what needs to be done. It also gives a common basis from which you can respond to the unexpected and unplanned, as will almost always occur on an activity of any complexity. This is a powerful basis with which to start a change initiative.

brilliant tip

What is systemic alignment?

In this chapter, and elsewhere in this book I use the word 'systemic'. It is not a word everyone is familiar with, so I want to give a short explanation. The *Oxford English Dictionary* (2nd edition) defines the word 'systemic' as an adjective meaning 'relating to a system, especially as opposed to a particular part'.

If you step back from the details, you can view the various aspects of your team combining into a system. In change situations we often need to take a systemic perspective – that is to think about the interconnections between different aspects of the team (e.g. the 'variable aspects' introduced in chapter 4), and how they interact as a system. Some of the biggest problems in change can arise by treating aspects as independent and not part of an integrated system. Another word that is sometimes used in this context is 'holistic'. I have avoided this word as it has a range of uses and connotations which I do not wish to make.

Systemic alignment is the consistent synchronisation of the different aspects of your team so they are all pulling in the same direction. For example, processes are consistent with IT systems, performance metrics are consistent with objectives, skills training is consistent with capability needs, etc.

If you are interested in thinking of teams and organisations as systems, you should look at *The Fifth Discipline: The Art and Practice of the Learning Organization* by Peter Senge. In this book he discusses the related concept of Systems Thinking and Systems Dynamics.

What needs to be done: understanding the work

Developing a plan starts with the identification of the work required. Usually the most sensible way of doing this is to start by identifying the main blocks of work that need to be undertaken. You can then break these large blocks of work down into ever smaller chunks until you have reached your desired level of detail. For change within a team, I generally work with a fairly high-level plan – one that is sufficient to understand the main sequence of activities, to allocate work out to team members and to identify the main dependencies between those activities.

In the last chapter we looked at deciding on your approach to change (e.g. which aspects to change, pursue radical or evolutionary change, focus on faults or focus on strengths, etc.). It is this approach you now need to convert into a plan. If you start by thinking about the change you have decided to pursue, it is normally straightforward to identify the main building blocks of work. One good way of doing this is to identify the elements of work in a short brainstorm with the people involved in the change initiative. The items you identify then need to be structured into a logical order, while considering any linkages or dependencies between them.

Brainstorming a change plan

If you are finding this brainstorming challenging, you can try the following method. Take four pieces of flip-chart paper, or draw four wide columns on a large whiteboard. I am going to ask you to trigger and group your ideas according to the logical ordering of the initiative. A typical initiative very roughly has:

- *A beginning:* this is when you design the change in detail and make sure the prerequisites are in place. *What things do you need to do before you can actively work on the change?*
- *A middle:* this is when you do the work needed to make the change. This can be anything from designing processes

to putting new desks in an office, from creating new jobs to building new IT functionality, from designing a new team structure to preparing to relocate a team. The list of work that a change could encompass is endless. Another way of thinking of this stage is the creation of the core mechanism for the change. *What are the mechanisms for your change?*

- *An implementation:* this is when the mechanism you have developed is implemented for real and becomes the basis for the work in your team. The team go from working in way A to working in way B. This is the critical point in change, and is discussed in more detail below. Taking the examples above – the team starts using the new desks, you fill the new roles, you use the new IT functionality, the team adopts the new structure or the team is relocated to the new location. *How will you actually implement your change?*

- *An end:* this is the phase post-implementation when any residual problems are resolved, and any remaining details completed. This can be a time for more vigilance than people expect – the change is not over until you are sure it will be sustained. *How will you complete your change and ensure it is sustained?*

The point of these four groups of activities is not to develop a plan which literally has four phases as indicated above, but to help stimulate the flow of ideas in your brainstorm (see Figure 5.1).

Once you have created a list of activities you are ready to start to structure them into a plan. The process of structuring the tasks into a plan will normally make you identify further activities to include.

An important step in designing a change plan is to determine all the interrelationships between the variable aspects of your team that you are modifying and the variable aspects which at this time you are not seeking to alter. A classic example is

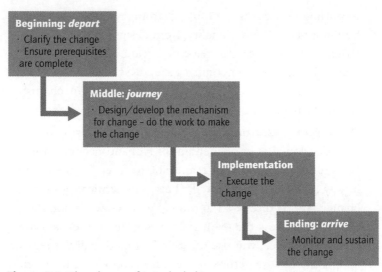

Figure 5.1 The phases of a typical change

the enhancement of an IT system. Rarely can this be done as a standalone change – normally it will require staff training and changes to working processes. Sometimes it will require changes to organisation and job roles. Taking a systemic view of your team is critical when it comes to change. Identifying and planning the necessary work on the linkages and interdependencies between different components makes a critical difference between a smooth and a troublesome change.

Five pillars of a successful change programme

I'll give you another tip for planning. When I am engaged to help an organisation with a change project of any sort, I look for five pillars which I regard as critical to successful change (see Figure 5.2). These are not planning tasks as such, but can help you think about the way you develop your plan. The five pillars are:

1   ***Story:*** this is the development, effective communication and evolution of a compelling vision for the outcome of the change programme. This typically includes *why* it is being

done, *why now – why* it is being done *now, what* needs to be done and *how* it will be undertaken. Does your plan include the activities to develop, maintain and communicate your story and other messages?

2 **Structure:** this is the project management approach of scoping, building a plan, allocating responsibility, tracking and driving progress and so on, which gives structure and purpose to your team's work. It makes their work effective and efficient. This chapter is largely concerned with initiating these tasks.

3 **Governance:** the effective steering and decision-making processes. Change programmes usually throw up a series of important decisions. Does your plan include the activities to put in place the necessary decision-making forums and the arrangements for these forums to meet?

4 **Systemic alignment:** which refers to how generally aligned your team is with the goals of your change programme. This may involve factors outside of the change programme that can influence its success. This is an element that some people struggle to understand, and yet when they see examples it becomes obvious. I will return to systemic alignment repeatedly in later chapters, but for now a simple example should be sufficient: if you want your team to work in some new way you should seek out and remove anything that gives them an incentive not to work in this way – for instance, the performance management system must be aligned with the change. *Are your staff bonused and rewarded for working in the way the change requires?* Does your plan include an assessment of the systemic impacts of your proposed change and actions to ensure alignment?

5 **Stakeholders:** the effective management and utilisation of stakeholder responses to the programme. Stakeholder

management is an important aspect of change management. When you are dealing with change solely within your team it is usually a lesser burden than on a complex multifunctional change programme. However it is still worth considering and we will touch on it below. Does your plan include the appropriate level of stakeholder management activity?

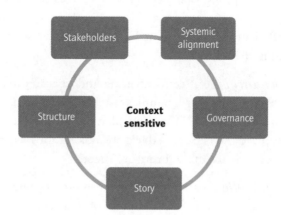

Figure 5.2 The pillars of successful change

We will talk about each of these in the following chapters. Change initiatives which have the best basis for success have certain characteristics. They are supported by a compelling story, a clear structure and process for maintaining that structure. They have effective governance and stakeholder management processes. There is also a level of systemic alignment between the goals of the change and the environment in which it is being implemented.

One other factor worth considering on top of this is contextual sensitivity – that is the appropriateness and acceptability of the approach for the situation. If you and your team are implementing your own change this is not normally an issue. Contextual sensitivity is most important when outside parties such as consultants, systems integrators, and contractors are being used to drive a change.

From task to outcomes

One of the tendencies with planning is to become intensely focussed on tasks. In some ways this is not surprising. It is in the nature of plans that they contain tasks. But you will not be thanked or rewarded for delivering a change initiative that is simply a set of completed tasks. Those tasks must lead to a beneficial outcome.

As you plan, you need to determine:

● What measures of performance will be affected by this change initiative?

● What degree of improvement is expected to be achieved by this change?

You should have started to think about this when you chose your approach to change. There is a huge range of performance improvements that change initiatives can result in. They can impact cost, quality of work, efficiency, throughput, risk, staff satisfaction, customer engagement and so on. Some of the most dramatic of change initiatives can be those that result in significant changes to the types of performance metrics an organisation measures.

In planning you should be thinking through the linkage between the tasks you are identifying and the desired outcome. The thought that should always be in your mind is: *will these tasks lead to the outcome that is needed?*

It is worth spending some time really considering in some depth the performance metrics the change will affect. These performance metrics are both the measure of success, but will also become a lever to help drive the change itself. As noted above the alignment of performance metrics with change goals is essential to success.

Timing and other constraints

Before you can turn the identified work into a plan you should consider whether you are operating under any specific constraints. The first and most common constraint is timing.

Planning exercises have a habit of implying timescales for a change initiative which are much longer than you desire. You may have specific times by which a change needs to be completed, either because some other event in the organisation is dependent on it, or simply because you have made a commitment to your boss that the change will be completed by a certain date.

Do not panic if your first cut plan does not meet your desired timescales, they rarely do. You now have to try and work out if the tasks in the plan can be completed in a quicker way. There are many approaches to this which an experienced project manager will know – such as cutting dependencies, increasing parallel working and time-boxing activities. Usually a plan's duration can be significantly reduced by creative thinking. But no amount of planning will make the impossible possible. If your planning really shows a change really cannot be done within a desired timescale, do not just ignore this and push on. Many managers have got their fingers burnt trying this!

> if a change cannot be done within a desired timescale, do not just ignore this and push on

Another timing issue relates to the fact that there may be some periods in your year when you do not want to implement changes. Change always risks disruption and there may be normal cyclical peaks in workload when you do not want to simultaneously risk making changes. A good example is for finance departments. Finance teams normally have to close the books at month, quarter and year end. Year end is the most critical of these. Few finance departments favour making changes to finance systems at that time of year.

A different timing constraint relates to decision makers. If you need key decisions or approvals to be made during your programme, what is the right forum and when does it meet? If you need to refer to some pre-existing senior committee or board, normally they will have an existing schedule of meetings you will have to conform to. This schedule needs to be built into your plan.

Timing is just one of a number of constraints upon your plan. There may be other changes going on in parallel which you have to account for or which you cannot disrupt. You may have limited resources to apply to a specific change, fewer than you ideally need or you may be missing some key skill set which can compromise or lengthen your plan. You may have budget limitations. You may also work in an organisation with a limited appetite for risk – which may reduce your opportunity to undertake certain changes or certain approaches to change. There may be impacts from the wider environment and organisation you work in. The key point is that a plan has to reflect not a theoretical view of how you might like to pursue your change, but a practical view of how you will pursue your change taking account all the different real-world factors that impact your team.

Stakeholders, decisions and approvals

A critical element in successful change is the identification, engagement and management of stakeholders. 'Stakeholder' is one of those words which has become an everyday part of management talk, yet it has not really been around for that long as a part of common speech. There are many definitions of stakeholder. A simple one, which is good enough, is that a stakeholder is *anyone who is affected by or can affect your change initiative*.

Stakeholder management at its highest level includes two activities. The first is utilising those people who support the change to provide backing for the change initiative. You are looking to develop a strong supporting coalition for your change. If the change is within the confines of your team then this support is mainly about gaining the support of key team members. If the change extends beyond your team, then you need a broader coalition. The second activity is to mitigate any unhelpful responses from those who are opposed to the change.

For a change within a team the stakeholders are primarily your team, probably your boss and other teams which you interface into and which are affected by the change. But this really depends on the nature of the change. You will also need support from specialist functions such as HR, IT or finance for some changes.

Stakeholder management consists of the activities of identifying, assessing, determining and prioritising appropriate actions and engaging stakeholders. Stakeholder management is always an important element in change and therefore needs to be built into your plan. Stakeholder management in relation to your direct team is covered in chapter 7.

My experience of stakeholder management in practice is very variable. Many teams focus on 'doing the work' – that is the core tasks of developing the change, and have a tendency to avoid what they see as 'office politics'. You will not get far in your management career unless you engage in office politics. It does not have to be self-serving or distasteful. Much of office politics is simply a natural reflection of work with people who have different interests. Human beings are political animals. Successful change almost always requires some degree of structured stakeholder management.

Stakeholder management needs to be taken seriously, but for a change within a team it should not become an industry in its own right. If you apply my definition of stakeholder you can easily end up with a massive list. This is where you need to balance perfect stakeholder management with pragmatism. For team-based change your most important audience is the team itself. In many cases you will have a small circle of external stakeholders you need to consider. You will need to set boundaries limiting the stakeholders that you really worry about. There are no universal rules to do this – it is a matter of balancing the risk of damaging your change initiative versus the time and effort you will spend managing the stakeholders. A sensible approach is to:

1   Determine a list of stakeholders (brainstorming is a good way to develop a first-cut list).

2   Remove those stakeholders whose interests are peripheral or who have minimal opportunity to support your cause.

3   Group together those stakeholders with similar interests and needs.

4   Prioritise the stakeholders you are going to invest in managing. Focus your efforts on these stakeholders.

Your key tool for stakeholder management is communication. This is dealt with in chapter 8.

Decision makers

One specific group of stakeholders you will need to pay close attention to are any decision makers or approvers with regard to your change. What, if any, approvals do you require outside of your team? You may not need any – but if you do require authorisation you need to think through how you will gain the necessary approvals to initiate the change, and how you will keep on gaining them as you go through the change. The general term often used for the activities relating to steering, decision making and approval on change initiatives is governance.

Two factors, I think, need particular attention with regard to decision makers. The first is that people do not always like being presented with a decision which they must make then and there. They want time to assess the decision, to mull it over and possibly to seek guidance from other people. Therefore, when you structure any appropriate governance mechanism into your plan think through not just the points when you need decisions – but also the buy-in and engagement process with those decision makers.

The second factor to build into your plan is the logistics for decision makers. Sometimes you need to call upon senior decision makers. Never forget such people have their own complex logistics and usually very limited time in their diaries to meet you. More than one change programme I have been involved in has run into trouble because it forgot to consider the logistics of key decision makers. For instance, occasionally you may need the support of the main board of the organisation for particularly large or radical changes. Such a body will not typically meet your timescale, but your timescale must be built around their existing schedule of meetings – taking account of administrative details such as how far in advance papers must be submitted for review.

If you can avoid such high-level decision-making forums it will generally make your life easier, but at some point in your career you probably will have to work with them. If you do, coordinate your logistics with their schedules as early as possible into your plan as it can have a significant impact on phasing and timing of the initiative.

Who will do what: roles and resources

Let me assume at this point you have an outline plan for your change initiative, and it includes all the tasks you need to perform to successfully achieve your plan. The next question is who will do which tasks? How will you allocate the work in the plan out across your team? What help do you need and what resources are available?

In truth, few of us develop a plan completely separately from considering who will do what work. You will usually be aware from the start of at least some of the people who will work on the initiative. But I think it is important to try and develop your understanding of the work before getting too bogged down in who will do it. The reason is that once you start thinking about people there is a tendency to start shaping the work to the people rather than worrying about what really needs to be done. As you think about resources you will almost always need to make compromises in your plan – but this should be done as a deliberate activity with awareness of the consequences, rather than the accidental result of who you allocate.

Once you start to really think about the people you have to do the work described in the plan two typical problems emerge. The first is that you will not have all the resources to do the work. Your team members have a day job, and are usually not sitting around waiting for additional change initiatives to pursue. Secondly, even if you have the raw headcount with sufficient time available to do the work, they may not have the skills.

There is no simple answer to these problems. You must spend some time iterating between the lists of tasks and your expected timescale, and the reality of the resources you have available. In the end, the plan has to reflect the resources you have for the change.

> the plan has to reflect the resources you have for the change

If you are missing resources you may be able to call on the help of other teams providing that you have a good relationship with them. This is worth exploring, but don't rely on it. Even with a supportive culture (which not all organisations have), few other teams will be in a different position from you. They will mostly be resource constrained as well. Alternatively, your organisation may have specialist functions such as teams of project and change managers to help with such initiatives. Experience shows such teams tend to be very busy and mostly focussed on the larger organisational changes. If you have the available budget, you may be able to bring contractors or consultants on board. This can be a good solution, but I recommend you do not exclusively use temporary staff to implement changes. Your team will learn nothing, it can create barriers to acceptance, and the change risks being insensitive to the contextual factors. However, a few skilled externals in key roles during your change can strengthen the team significantly without creating these problems.

A constructive approach is to look at a change initiative as an opportunity for team members to develop new skills. Change initiatives are often intense learning experiences, and a brilliant way to gain some on-the-job training. You do have to be realistic about quite how far you can stretch your team members. But if you are willing to invest some of your own time coaching team members on the change initiative then you will find many members of your team will rise to the challenge. Occasionally, you will have a training budget to provide some change management training. This is ideal, but don't become obsessed with formal training. Many successful changes have been driven by people with no formal change management training.

When allocating team members to the change initiative you need to consider the core work required to achieve the change, the activities associated with coordinating this work, the activities that provide encouragement to staff through the change, and dealing with issues that arise. In other words, you need someone to lead the change. This may be you, but it does not need to be. In fact, it is often beneficial to separate the role of line manager from the change leader for a specific change initiative. You have a major role to play in the change whether or not you are the day-to-day leader of this specific change.

Whichever approach you choose, the bottom line is that change will not happen unless you are willing to allocate sufficient resources. For any significant change this will almost always have an impact on the normal operational performance of the team. This is discussed more in chapter 6.

The critical point: implementation of change

At some point in every change initiative comes the time that the change is implemented: a team goes from working in an original state A to a new improved way of working in state B. This is often the highest risk step of any change initiative.

The point at which a change is being implemented is usually the first time you will find out if it works as you expected it to. During the change, teams can find themselves working partially in old state A and partially in new state B – or worse, having to do work twice, once in the old way and once in the new way. Implementation of change is associated with many risks and occasionally catastrophic failures. There is even a special section of planning – implementation planning and transition planning to deal with these circumstances, and the specialist role of transition planner used on some of the more complex organisational changes. This critical point of your change initiative needs careful planning.

brilliant tip

Implementation or transition

I tend to use the words 'implementation' and 'transition' whenever discussing the stage at which a change is applied to a team. Both words are in common usage in business, but they have slightly different meanings. Other related words include 'cutover' and 'go-live'.

Implementation is the more general term which refers to all the activities of applying a change to a team. Care is needed when

▶

using this word. Sometimes the word 'implementation' is applied to a whole plan. In this sense it means executing the whole plan (the beginning, middle, implementation and end stages). This is in contrast to implementing the change – that is executing a specific stage of the plan. In this book, I use the word implementation to refer specifically to the stage of applying the change.

Transition is a specific form of implementation. It implies that the change cannot be applied in one instant, but will be achieved gradually over a period of time. Most changes require a period of transition as a change is rarely achievable in an instant. Some aspects of change may be effectively instantaneous – for example, the switch-off of an old IT system. Even so, there is usually a period of transition as team members learn the new ways of working fully. During the transition phase the team will be partially working in old ways and partially working in new. Also during the transition phase, performance of the team typically dips as they get used to the new ways of working – but this depends on the approach taken.

As a team leader you need to be aware of and cautious of the implementation phase, but you should not be paranoid. Yes some changes have significant risks associated with them, but the largest risks are normally related to big organisational changes and not the changes you will run into within your team. If you are part of a larger organisational change, then the overall change leader should be worrying about the implementation phase. However, it is always worth checking the implementation approach being proposed – as it is often operational and 'coal-face' team leaders rather than programme managers who understand best how their teams can adapt to the process of changing.

There are a number of factors you should consider with regard to transition for your change. The relevance of these factors does

depend on context, and you will have to decide whether you
need to consider them or not – the key factor in that decision
is the level of risk to business-as-usual work from the change
implementation. Considerations in assessing this risk are:

- **What is the impact of a drop in the team's business-as-usual performance?** In some situations the work
  of your team may be critical to the minute-by-minute
  operations of the organisation as a whole. Then there can
  be no drop in performance during the change. In other
  situations, while your team's role is important, if work
  stops for a few days the wider organisation will continue to
  operate smoothly. Depending on where your team sits on
  this spectrum you can take more or less risk during change
  implementation.

- **What is the appropriate phasing of the change?**
  There are many ways of implementing change, which have
  different risk, resource and timing profiles. At one extreme
  is the big-bang approach when a change is implemented
  in its entirety at once. This is normally quick, but can
  be risky. Changes can be phased into a series of smaller
  implementations. This extends the duration but reduces risk,
  and you have the opportunity to learn and improve each
  phase of implementation. Or there can be some form of
  transition as the change is gradually implemented and the
  team spends some time in parallel running, using both the
  old and the new ways of working. This is low risk, but can
  be very intense on your team, working in two ways at once.

- **Can you break the change into smaller chunks?**
  Generally it is easier to adapt to several smaller changes
  than one large change. Sometimes this is not possible, but
  it is worth reviewing whether you can break the change into
  smaller, easier to swallow, pieces. If you can, and it does not
  add too much to the duration of your change, then often
  this is the best way.

- *What will you do if the change fails?* Can you revert or rollback to previous ways of working? This is not something you need to consider on all changes, but some changes have such a critical impact on the operation of your team that if they fail for any reason you will be unable to perform some key area of work. You should consider how you can minimise the risks of this happening with testing prior to change implementation. You should also consider how you can unravel or reverse the change post-implementation.

- *Are there any other appropriate ways of reducing transition risk?* There are numerous ways of reducing transition risk – for example, planning transition at times when your workload is low and keeping a buffer of resources for that time to ensure problems can be resolved. Consider what, if any, additional risk mitigation you should build into your plan.

Review the plan

The final part of planning is to review the plan. In reviewing the plan you should be doing a common-sense check, asking yourself:

- Will this plan achieve the expected change? Does that include achieving the necessary level of performance improvement?

- Does the plan make the best balance of time, resource, cost and risk to achieve this change?

- Does the plan encompass all the necessary work? Are there any gaps and omissions in the plan?

- Does the plan account for the dependencies between tasks?

- Has the systemic alignment of this change with other components of your team (or external to your team) been thought through?

- Are there any other external factors, such as commitments or key organisation events, that the plan needs to account for?
- Does your plan take account of decision-maker availability and logistics?
- Is the implementation or transition approach appropriate for this change?
- Does this plan take a realistic view of the way your organisation works, how things get done and how long they take?

You should hold in mind the gap between where you are and where you want to be. If you execute this plan will it take you on the journey you want to go on and will it get you where you want to get? You probably cannot categorically answer this question, but you need to feel comfortable that within a normally acceptable level of risk your plan is the right approach. If you think so, you are ready. If not, you need to spend some more time planning. You cannot plan forever, but do not be too impatient to get out of the planning cycle – it will pay dividends in the end.

Raising plan problems with your boss

As a result of your review you may find that you cannot complete the change within the expectations of your boss. You may feel you need additional resources, funding or some consideration to be taken of its likely impact on operational work. This means you need to go back to your boss or other stakeholder and manage their expectations.

There is an art in raising problems with delivering change without sounding as if you are a weak manager or a 'whinger'. If you think there are real problems with the change then it is important you do flag them. I have seen too many gung-ho managers who have leapt into changes with insufficient resources or a failure to take account of the impact on their normal work, who have ended up regretting it. But there are ways of flagging problems that can result in esteem for you rising, and other ways which can sound like lack of imagination, drive or ambition.

The plan helps. If you have gone to the trouble of developing a full plan, if you have thought about the systemic impacts of your proposed change, its effect on your resources and on normal operational performance levels, you have a strong fact base on which to make a reasoned argument. You then stand a much better chance of a constructive response in understanding your problems, help in resolving them, or relief in the normal levels of service your team provides while the change is ongoing.

brilliant recap

Successful change, especially change of larger scale, risk or complexity, benefits from appropriate levels of planning. It is the planning process, as much as the creation of the plan as an artefact, which enables team members to develop a robust and shared understanding of what needs to be done.

Planning starts by identifying the chunks of work that need to be done. Think broadly when planning for change. Change initiatives which have the best basis for success have certain characteristics. They are supported by a compelling story, a clear structure and process for maintaining that structure. They have effective governance and stakeholder management processes. There is also a level of systemic alignment between the goals of the change and the environment in which it is being implemented. Your plan should also take account of change implementation – namely, how to mitigate the risks associated with the transition to the new ways of working.

Planning may start as a theoretical exercise, but soon has to become a practical basis for the work, taking account of real-world factors such as time and cost constraints, the availability and skills of the people in your team to work on the change, and risk.

Having developed a plan, you should always do a common-sense check to satisfy yourself that the plan which your team will embark on is an effective and efficient approach that will achieve the goals of your change.

CHAPTER 6

Change and do the day job

With your plan, you are now in a position to start to implement your change. At its simplest this is a matter of following your plan until the change is completed. But there are good ways and bad ways of following a plan. In this chapter I describe the switch from planning to active work on the change, and how to deliver against the plan. This must all be done within the context of the business-as-usual work your team does. Change may be important, but rarely is it so important you can stop doing the day job.

Mobilise the change initiative

Delivering change results from taking action. You have a plan which describes the action to be taken, and now the people who will work on the change initiative need to start work. Often this is as simple as you instructing them to start work. For some more complex changes you may need a mobilisation or kick-off meeting.

At the kick-off you review the vision and plan for the change. One aim is to make sure everyone knows their role, knows how their work interrelates with that of other people working on the change and understands how the work will be coordinated. Another aim of a kick-off meeting is to instil enthusiasm for the change amongst the team members involved. It is also worth outlining any working rules or guiding principles.

An important guiding principle must be that business-as-usual work will continue to be delivered. While teams will be under

pressure to make improvements, the team whose normal operational performance drops every time a change is implemented
will be criticised and come under pressure to improve it. As a
manager you must try to keep everyone doing what they are
normally meant to do. There are limits to this because change
is inherently disruptive, and some of your team will be working
on the change initiative and not doing their normal work. Later
on in this chapter I discuss how to mitigate this problem and
appropriately manage expectations.

As part of kick-off, roles in the change should be clarified – in
other words, who does what. One important role is your own.
The team involved in the change needs to understand what level
of involvement you intend to take. Will you be actively engaged
in the change, part of the change team or even the change
leader, or will you take a more hands-off role, expecting periodic
updates and acting more like a project sponsor? It is helpful to
be clear about this – you do not want to get to the situation in
which the change initiative stalls because everyone is waiting
for you to do something, when in fact you were not planning
to be involved in that way. On the other hand, you probably do
not want the team making significant decisions without some
involvement from you. Clarity about your role and the level of
authority you delegate to the change team is important. If you
have a good team, my advice is not to be afraid to take a relatively hands-off engagement with significant discretionary power
for those working on the initiative. In most cases, team leaders
who show trust in their teams are rewarded with good performance. Sometimes this requires giving a little more space than the
leader is naturally comfortable with.

Beyond clarifying your formal role on the change, you should
prepare yourself for the journey. In a change of any significance,
you need to be ready to support it at all times with your behaviour, the things you say, your enthusiasm, and a willingness to
devote time to the change as and when required.

Progress the plan

Anyone who has ever followed a project plan, especially a plan for change, will tell you plans are never perfect. Having a plan helps you work through the change, but a plan needs active management. There are many reasons for this, but they all come down to the fact that none of us has flawless foresight. Things will occur during a change initiative which have not been predicted, obstacles will transpire and unexpected responses to the change will arise.

A plan should not therefore be regarded as an invariable script. It is more a tool which helps to show the direction, but which in itself needs to be monitored and maintained. The monitoring and maintenance of the plan may be done by you, or by the person you have appointed to lead the change. The better your plan, the easier your life will be, but never treat the plan as a sacrosanct statement of the truth. One good way of thinking about this is in terms of an ongoing plan–do–review cycle. You plan, you do some of the work, you review where you are, and then the plan is updated. This cycle continues all the way through your change.

> you plan, you do some of the work, you review where you are, and then the plan is updated

Effective regular reviews need someone to closely monitor the change initiative as it progresses. In monitoring you should be thinking at three levels, which I call task, delivery and outcome.

1 *Task:* Are you doing the things you expected to be doing – i.e. following the plan? This requires a plan which you can follow and which team members' activities clearly relate to.

2 *Delivery:* Is completing the tasks resulting in production of the deliverables you expected (i.e. new processes, IT systems, training – or whatever else is being changed)?

3 ***Outcome:*** Is the use of the deliverables resulting in the outcomes you expected? This requires you to have performance measures which you track and see the trend in as the change progresses.

The logic of this is straightforward. You do things that result in something being produced, and by using or applying what you have produced you achieve an outcome. Good management of a change initiative requires thinking at each of the levels of task, delivery and outcome. This is at the core of thinking like a project manager. (There is a fourth level, which is only realised over time. This is the realisation of benefits – these four levels are shown in Figure 6.1.)

The basis for review is the information you get by monitoring your progress relative to the plan. By monitoring progress you can work out how much progress you are making, and what needs to be done to keep your change on track. The difficulty of monitoring depends on the scale and complexity of the change. Typically, checking activity progress – have people done what the plan suggests – is the easiest. Checking outcome progress – is it leading to the result you wanted, and knowing that any alteration in performance is actually due to the change – is the most difficult.

Figure 6.1 Task-delivery-outcome-benefits

Deal with problems

Treat the execution of the plan as a learning opportunity, not a test of how accurate your planning was. Of course, if you are undertaking a form of change you are familiar with you should expect your plan to be reasonably accurate. But when you undertake a novel or innovative change, the likelihood is that your plan will be at best approximately accurate. You will find omissions in the plan and you will have incorrectly estimated the time and cost of certain activities. This is normal. The skill in managing change is rarely about perfect planning. It is about how you deal with problems.

> the skill in managing change is rarely about perfect planning – it is about how you deal with problems

If problems are to be dealt with quickly and effectively they need to be flagged as soon as anyone is aware of them. You should avoid creating a culture in which people are afraid to admit to planning mistakes. If you are the type of manager who tends to shout and scream, or find ways of penalising people whenever a problem arises – try to resist this urge. It will rarely result in better planning, but it will result in people trying to hide mistakes, which is unlikely to be helpful.

It is not unreasonable for you to expect your team to get better at planning and estimating changes of a type they regularly undertake. Positive and constructive feedback will help with this (as will reviewing, as we discuss in chapter 9). If it is important for your plan to be accurate and your team do not have experience in this type of change, then you should seek external expert assistance.

You should encourage people to admit mistakes in either the approach you are taking or the content of your plan. Issues that arise should be identified, analysed and assessed – and action taken. That action may be to task an individual or sub-team with some specific set of activities to resolve the problem, or it may be by amending the plan. The most important point at this stage is that problems are resolved quickly. Stick to constructive feedback to maintain engagement and willingness to be open about potential future problems. This is all part of developing a positive change culture.

One of the most significant challenges you will come across on change initiatives is the need to deal with your team members' reactions to change. This topic is discussed in chapter 7.

The approach I am suggesting may sound unacceptably fluid and imprecise for some people, but it reflects the sometimes untidy nature of change initiatives. If you really need to work to committed timescales and costs for a change, the answer may be to spend more time in detailed planning, but I am sceptical that, unless you have deep expertise in a type of change, such planning will provide you with a truly accurate plan. A more realistic answer is to build a plan with sufficient leeway or contingency in it to respond to the unexpected. The other answer is to seek a real commitment from your team to deliver the change within the necessary time or cost. You will often be pleasantly surprised by how much a well-motivated team can deliver in a short period of time, even if the plan is imperfect.

Maintain the plan

A plan is your best view of how things will go at a point in time. Then reality occurs and your plan will soon become out of date. Plans need to be refreshed and updated through the life of the change initiative. At periodic intervals update the plan to your best current understanding. The frequency of these updates depends on the pace of work. Some forms of project management seek very frequent updates to plans, others make it infrequent. On a team change initiative I typically seek to revise plans on a monthly basis – but it depends on the scale and duration of the change initiative.

By formally revising the plan you can both review what action you need to take to keep an initiative on track, and you also have a basis for expectations to be managed.

Keep doing the day job

One of the most important lessons I have learnt time and time again with regard to implementing change is that managers have to ensure their team keeps doing the day job. Those business-as-usual activities that your team exists to perform still need to carry on during change. Work must be completed, customers need to be satisfied and your boss needs to continue to feel that all is under control. Unfortunately, change initiatives have a habit of getting in the way of everyday work. In this section I look at four major risks to business-as-usual activity during change, and suggest ways you can deal with this.

brilliant tip

Your everyday work

There are various ways of referring to the normal work your team performs outside of the change initiative - *the day job, business-as-usual, operational work* and so on. Different organisations favour different terms. I switch between all three in this book.

Capacity and the availability of key staff

The first area a change initiative will affect is team members' availability to do the business-as-usual work of your team. For example, if you remove 20 per cent of the people to work on the change initiative you evidently will have roughly 20 per cent less capacity to do the normal work. Most teams have a certain buffer of spare capacity, and it is not normally a direct equivalence of losing capacity of X per cent and therefore reducing work done by X per cent. Nevertheless, unless you are in the unusual situation of running a team with spare capacity, if you move people to a change initiative, the throughput of business-as-usual work will drop. What can you do about this?

The first thing most managers try to do is to get the rest of the team to pick up the slack. This can be a solution for the short term, but rarely is a viable long-term prospect. Unless you have particularly attractive overtime payments or other induce-ments to do additional work, most people will sooner or later start to resent the additional work they are doing while others are unavailable. It will be regarded as unfair. In situations with tense or difficult industrial relations it can even lead to industrial action. Fortunately this is rare, but you do need to be reasonable about how much additional work the remaining team can pick up. Certainly as a short-term fix you may be able to ask team members temporarily to pick up the work not performed by their colleagues, but rarely will this be effective for more than a few weeks.

The second typical response is to try and get some 'backfill' – that is, someone else to do the work you do not now have the team members to do. Typically, you will employ staff on short-term contracts. This can be effective, but suffers from two major problems. The first is a budgetary issue of finding the additional money for the contract staff. The second is that the contract staff are usually not as productive as the staff you have allocated to the change project, because they do not know the work and their way around the organisation so well.

If you need an extra budget for backfill staff, then the best approach is to try and build it into the business case for the change. If the change initiative's business case cannot bear this cost then it is probably not the right change to be pursuing. However, even if you have a strong case, requests for backfill are often rejected. Try, but don't bank on it being approved.

If a budget is available, one decision managers often face in this situation is whether to backfill normal operational roles or instead to staff the change initiative with contractors or consultants and so avoid the drain on business-as-usual work. The answer does depend on the context, but I normally favour using contract staff to backfill, rather than using contractors on the change initiative itself. Backfill is a temporary measure and any problems in using contractors will be short term. However, you may live for a long time with the changes delivered by consultants. For many reasons it is better if they are designed and worked on by your own team members. If you need specific expertise to be introduced to change initiatives, then use external consultants or contractors, but they should be a minority of the team.

> use external consultants or contractors, but they should be a minority of the team

The third response to capacity problems is to accept the drop in capacity and just to do less work for the duration of the change initiative. I always recommend against simply treating the drop in performance as an unavoidable result of a change initiative. You have choices as a manager, for example to reprioritise your team to focus on the highest priority work. Rarely is all the work your team does of the same value. Focus on the highest value while your capacity is constrained. However you allocated your limited resources, if you are going to reduce the level of work the team does, you should manage the expectations of your own boss and customers carefully.

The three options outlined here are not mutually exclusive, and the best solution often lies in a combination of all three: some short-term increase in work by the remaining team, some backfill for key roles and some carefully timed reduction in throughput aligned with cautiously managed expectations.

Rubber-necking: the change as the focus of interest

Change initiatives can be interesting, especially to those not involved. Change initiatives may be a source of concern for members of the team, worrying about the impact of the change on them. Change initiatives will be the source of gossip and rumour. The end result of this is that members of your team can cease focussing on their day job and start obsessively looking out for, worrying about and chatting about the change initiative. As a result productivity drops. This habit of team members taking their eyes off the ball is analogous to drivers 'rubber-necking' when they see something of interest on the road.

This is human nature, and while the drop in productivity may be unwelcome, it is natural for people to be interested and concerned about change if they think it may affect them directly. If there is a strong and trusting relationship between you and the team you may be able to minimise this by telling people they have nothing to worry about. In most cases this will not be enough, and should only be done if there really is nothing to worry about. If you damage your team's trust in you on this occasion then you will struggle on future change initiatives when trust is required. It is rarely worth damaging your trust with your team for a short-term benefit.

You can keep the team focussed on their normal work by tight management and holding people to account for achieving the agreed levels of performance. But if you show a heightened interest in performance levels just during change initiatives, you risk leaving a bad taste in your team's mouth, and it can result in doubt about how benign the changes really are.

The best way to keep team members who are not involved in the change initiative focussed on their normal work is to be as open as you can about the change. Keep them informed about goals, status, decision points and progress. There will be times that you cannot do this, but those occasions should be relatively few and far between. Even then, you can assuage concerns by giving a schedule of days when you can give them more information.

Knock-on impacts of change

I have mentioned several times in this book that organisations are complex, and the aspects or components that form part of a team are rarely fully independent. Driving change can be like trying to pull a thread from a piece of clothing: if you are not careful you can unexpectedly unravel more of the cloth than expected. As you change one component in your team you will sometimes find an unexpected impact elsewhere.

The examples of this are legion. Change an IT system and another that it interfaces with can fall over. Remove some data which you thought was not relevant and you may find some critical report no longer being delivered at the end of the year. Increase one person's salary or benefits and you can end up with challenges to make equivalent changes to other people's benefits. There are numerous examples of the way your team and the components of processes, IT applications, tools, facilities and so on work as an integrated system.

There is no totally reliable way around these sorts of risks. Experience and a deep understanding of how your department works are one way to minimise such risks. This is a key reason why when experienced people seem to you to be moaning about the change you should listen to their words rather than just the tone. Sometimes the complaints, which you may be tempted to ignore, will be based on important facts and implications you were unaware of. Additionally, process documentation, systems architecture diagrams and other representations of how aspects of your team hang together can help you identify such issues. In some areas, such as software development, there are testing stages – for example, regression testing – which are undertaken specifically to ensure that what is changed fits into the wider environment. But in the end you will also have to rely on vigilance and rapid response to problems that arise as you undertake the change.

Other important forms of risk you must account for are implementation risk or transition risk. These risks relate to the actual phase in a change initiative when a change is implemented, and a team transitions from working in one way to another way. There are many factors to consider in deciding when and how to implement change. The transition from one state to another, when a team may be partially working in the original state A and partially in the new state B, can be one of the highest risk phases of a change – especially if it is complex. This topic was discussed in chapter 5.

Management focus

The last way a change initiative can affect business-as-usual performance is in your personal focus. The change initiative may be very important to you. Changes will sometimes be large and complex – and this can mean that they require lots of your time to support them. Changes can be interesting. It is often much more interesting to be thinking about the future than doing what may seem in comparison to be the mundane business-as-usual work. The change is the future, and while it is important, you get paid for your output today.

If you have a strong self-managing and self-motivating team, then it may be possible for you to switch your attention away from the day job to the change initiative for prolonged periods of time. But if this is not true then you must find a way of maintaining management oversight and direction of business-as-usual work while you are supporting the change initiative. I have seen several highly talented managers fail, even though they were delivering innovative change, because operational performance dropped too much while they were focussing on the change.

If you think you must focus predominantly on the change, and if you think your team will not operate successfully without a manager, consider putting someone temporarily in your place. This may seem a radical solution, but it is better than letting performance drift downwards. You could ask one of your team to act as the team leader temporarily as a career development opportunity, or you could consider bringing someone else in, perhaps a contract manager, to run the team for a limited period of time.

Managing expectations

What differentiates the most successful managers when it comes to change and the average performers? Good vision, planning, risk management and control of initiative implementation seem to be important factors. However, I think there is one other key factor. I have not done a scientific study, but in my experience one of the key differentiators is the way they manage expectations.

Managing expectations is the process of providing information to various stakeholders in the change in such a way that what happens on the change initiative is what they expect to happen. By avoiding surprises and aligning what happens with what is

> by avoiding surprises and aligning what happens with what is anticipated you build credibility and trust

anticipated you build credibility and trust. Through managing expectations you try to avoid the risk of disappointing or annoying people you work with or whose relationships are important to the smooth functioning of your team.

During a change initiative there are two areas in which you have to manage expectations:

- *Expectations about the change itself:* which is mostly of interest to you and your team, but may also be important to your boss and a limited circle of other stakeholders. This includes explaining the impact of the change on the people in the team, the speed of change, and any issues relating to the cost of the change.

● ***Expectations about business-as-usual work:*** which is mostly of interest to your customers and others who depend on your work. This requires keeping people informed about any impact on your business-as-usual work from the change, how it can be mitigated and how long such impacts will last.

Managing expectations needs care with what you tell people when, but at its heart requires telling the truth, even if it is a rather tactical form of truth telling. When you try to manage people's expectations be honest and warn people up-front that, while you will predict as best you can and you will flag when problems arise, sometimes things will happen you have not predicted. If something goes wrong commit to trying to put it right as quickly as possible, and live by this commitment. The old mantra of 'under-promise and over-deliver' may be a simplification, but it is a very good rule of thumb.

Often when you want to initiate change you will be asked questions like 'can you guarantee that this change will have no impact on my department?', or 'can you promise you will not reduce performance levels while changing?'. These are usually unrealistic requests. Resist the temptation to promise that the process of change will have no visible impact and no temporary detrimental effects on anyone else. This is rarely, if ever, true. Such promises normally come back to haunt you. No one will like it when you refuse to make such promises, but they will like it even less if you make the promise and then fail to keep it. If you fail to keep such promises you will soon have people angrily pointing at you saying 'but you promised...' or 'you gave me a commitment that...'. (Some of your more scheming colleagues will ask for your commitment, knowing perfectly well you will not be able to keep it. When you fail, it will give them an excuse for their own failures. Devious, I know – but there are Machiavellian people out there!)

The best you can do is to promise to minimise any detrimental impacts and respond quickly if something bad occurs. If you really understand your team's work you may even be able to quantify the level of risk or scale of impact. No one expects perfection, but you should seek to avoid major surprises. If you can eliminate the minor ones too, your credibility will rise.

Managing stakeholder expectations can be time consuming, and that effort will not always be understood nor the result appreciated. If, as a result of this, you are tempted not to worry about managing expectations remember that trust is a valuable commodity that has to be earned. Managing expectations is core to building trust. Trust is fragile and easier to lose than to develop.

> managing expectations is core to building trust

Often you will end up working with the same people on future changes. Your stakeholder community may evolve over time, but in most organisations you and your team's primary stakeholders are fairly static. Therefore when you think about how you manage expectations, do not just think about this change, think about the long-term relationships you want to develop. You may not always see the benefits of managing expectations in the short run, but in the longer run it will pay dividends.

brilliant recap

Once a plan has been developed you are ready to execute the change. A good way to start this, especially for larger or more complex changes, is with a formal kick-off session.

Executing a change initiative means following the plan you have developed. You must execute the tasks and monitor the results. In monitoring the results you should be looking to check that you are making progress in terms of the tasks in the plan being completed, making progress in terms of those tasks creating the deliverables you require, and in the application of those deliverables leading to the change outcomes you intended.

Few teams have the luxury of forgetting their normal business-as-usual or operational work during change. The day job must keep being done, operational performance must be maintained. Change initiatives throw up four challenges to do the normal day job which you must work to mitigate:

- Resource constraints as a result of team members working on the change.
- Team members reducing focus on their normal work to observe and discuss the change.
- Systemic impacts of the change – that is, unexpected impacts of the change on related components of your organisation when you had not foreseen the linkage.
- Team leaders focussing too much on the change and not driving business-as-usual performance.

It's critically important in a successful change initiative to manage expectations carefully about the change and about any impact on business-as-usual work. Ideally what happens is what your stakeholders expect to happen.

CHAPTER 7

Adapting to and adopting change

At the core of change management are the activities of guiding, encouraging, helping and facilitating people to adapt to and to adopt change. In guiding change adoption you are seeking for individuals to behave or work in some way that is different from the way they worked before the change was made. Sometimes this alteration in behaviour is minor, such as using a different sequence of keys in an improved IT system. Sometimes this alteration in behaviour is major, such as a radical redesign of work associated with new job roles. In many situations the change results in a tangible physical modification – such as when a company launches new products or redesigns office layouts. In others, the change results in less tangible outcomes, such as shifting the focus or attitude of an organisation from individual performance to a greater emphasis on team work and cross-functional working.

Whatever form the change takes, the steps taken to support the adaptation to and adoption of change lie at the heart of change management. The aim is not merely to make a change happen at a point in time, but to sustain the alteration in behaviour. This is important to focus on, as without ongoing support changes have a habit of unravelling and old ways of work re-establishing themselves even after a new way has been implemented.

the steps taken to support the adaptation to and adoption of change lie at the heart of change management

The focus on change management is people – as individuals, as teams and across an organisation as a whole. As a team leader you are not directly concerned with the organisation in its entirety, but you should be deeply engaged with the change as it affects the individuals in your team and the team as a unit.

This chapter contains more references to theory and models which support change than the previous chapters. I have selected pieces of theory you may already be familiar with, but if not, rest assured that they are straightforward and practical. I have included them because they are helpful and because if you deal with change management professionals they may refer to these concepts.

brilliant tip

The different meanings of 'change management'

The phrase 'change management' has an ambiguous scope. Sometimes when people use it they mean the end-to-end process of change – from preparing for change, developing changes, implementing change and ensuring change is sustained. This is the way I have used the phrase so far in this book. An alternative use refers specifically to the activities associated with adopting and adapting to change – such as training, communications and overcoming resistance. This is a much more restricted scope. This chapter deals with change management in this secondary critical but restricted fashion.

One way of differentiating between these two related, but differently scoped, meanings is to call the former 'the management of change' and the latter 'change management'. I tried this for a while, but found it often confused the people I was working with.

In most situations, you do not need to be too specific about which meaning of change management you are using. But there are occasions when it is important to differentiate. For example, consider when you engage someone to act as a change manager on one of your initiatives. Are they being engaged to run the initiative from end to end, or to do the more focussed role of helping team members adapt to and adopt change?

Managing change

Change can seem awfully complex. This can result in confusion about how to approach it, and occasionally a management attitude of ignoring change management as being far too hard to worry about. It should not be this way. Change management has shown its value time and again in achieving sustained change in an effective and low-risk way. While the process of change can be multifaceted, it is straightforward to conceptualise and to build useful models of, and based on these conceptual models to lead and to manage. This process starts by thinking about individuals. How does an individual adapt to change, adopt a new style of behaviour and in doing so implement the change? There is lots of complexity in the precise way every single individual goes through change, but the experience in general terms is not difficult to understand.

The individual experiencing a change, to be able to personally adapt to the change, has to develop the following:

- An *awareness* that a change is occurring.
- An *understanding* of the change and its implications for them.
- The *capability* and skills to work in the way the change requires.
- A *willingness* to work in the new way.

You can also identify a fifth component associated with individual change, namely providing encouragement or a reason to change and an absence of significant obstacles to changing. For change to be successful, the encouragements to change should be more compelling than the obstacles.

These five components all need to be reflected in the design and planning of a change initiative. When change is broken down into these five components, it becomes evident that change initiatives require the following main categories of activity (see Figure 7.1):

● Communication and education to provide awareness and understanding of the change.

● Education and training to provide skills and capabilities to conform to the change.

● Encouragement and support to develop willingness to work in the new way.

● Assessment of the situation – leading to the identification and alleviation of obstacles and the creation of aids to enable individuals to work in the new way.

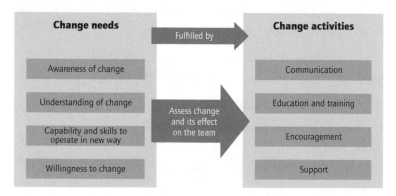

Figure 7.1 The basic elements that enable change

There are many factors that need to be accounted for when embarking on change. It can take time to understand and learn how to work in a new way. There are usually pressures both encouraging and resisting the change. Those encouraging the change should be leveraged – and those resisting should be reduced or countered. There are factors relating to systemic alignment which I have discussed in earlier chapters in this book. This can include practical issues such as the availability of the necessary tools and infrastructure to work in the new way. You must also consider the behaviour of the whole team. Is peer pressure likely to help or hinder the change? These points all reflect the need to try and look at change holistically, rather than as an isolated issue. Few things in modern integrated organisations can really be dealt with in total isolation.

Underlying this is the reality that you cannot force people to change. Adoption of and compliance with a change is something people choose to do. Of course, you have levers to encourage compliance – you can

> adoption of and compliance with a change is something people choose to do

penalise people in terms of benefits for not complying and in extremis even consider some type of formal censure such as a warning or even sacking. If you are thinking along these lines I suggest you take great care and try to find a more positive way of encouraging change. Change rarely works well if the reasons for change are all avoidance of penalty or punishment. People who accede to change for negative reasons have a tendency to pay lip service to the change and will do what they can to ignore or avoid the change. Forced change is not conducive to team and working relationships.

It is naive to expect that every change can be achieved purely on a positive basis – but it is far better when it can be. You should not be seeking cursory willingness to adopt a change. Willingness to work in compliance with a change is not a binary yes/no characteristic – there are levels of compliance. Your goal is to achieve a full and positive attitude to the change, and this normally requires positive reasons to change.

If you are tempted to try and force change through by mandate and using your power as the team leader, think about the long term. The success of change within a team is often a result of the history and experience of past changes. When you have been open, fair and worked with the team to understand issues and problems with a change, you are much more likely to develop a more trusting and willing attitude to future changes. If the history of changes has been one of forcing through unpleasant and difficult changes on an unwilling team, the chances are that future changes will be more difficult. Real-life factors, such as the economic situation and competitive pressures, means organisations sometimes need to pursue unpopular changes which are detrimental to the interests of some team members. You can still do this in a way that builds respect and trust. But this takes care and effort and it is easy in such situations to create bad long-term relationships.

The field force diagram

One simple way to think about the nature of change was developed by one of the founding fathers of change management, Kurt Lewin, when he came up with the concept of a field force diagram. In a field force diagram you can represent all the forces helping you make your change happen, and the restraining or resisting forces that get in the way. An example of a restraining force may be the expected negative response to a change from a key group you must work with. A driving force might be the active support of a senior executive who favours the change.

Field force diagrams are sometimes criticised as being too simplistic. They are simple, but still I find they are a useful and quick way of getting your head around the major issues in a change initiative. They are not an accurate quantitative tool, but generally you do not need this. By drawing up your own field force diagram you can create a simple, visual understanding of the challenge the change poses for you and your team. From this understanding you can think through the implications for your change initiative. An example of a simple field force diagram is shown in Figure 7.2.

In essence, change management involves thinking about the driving and restraining forces and working out how to use or overcome them. By considering these forces, you can identify a number of key steps in the change management features of your initiative. In outline, the main steps you need to take are:

1 Identify who is affected by the change.

2 Review:

   (a) Determine what the impact of change is on the identified community.

   (b) Predict and assess responses to change.

   (c) Identify obstacles and aids to change.

   (d) Assess the capability to change.

Figure 7.2 Field force diagram

3 Guide the change:

(a) Raise awareness and understanding of the change.

(b) Provide education and training for the change.

(c) Encourage and support the team to work in the new way.

(d) Overcome or mitigate any obstacles to change.

4 Monitor and respond:

(a) Assess how the change is progressing.

(b) Review and, if appropriate, modify your approach as the situation evolves.

Step 4 is important. Change can rarely be run as a simple logical ordering of steps. In reality, you will find yourself often repeating the steps as the reality of the change initiatives – and the responses to the change and the problems it throws up – unfold. For instance, some of your team members may learn a new way of working quickly, while others may take more time. Some of your team members may readily accede to a change, while others may vigorously oppose the change. In the course of a normal change you will find supporters and early adopters, stragglers and strugglers and some who resist.

> you will find supporters and early adopters, stragglers and strugglers and some who resist

Awareness, understanding and capability to change

A major part of the work in a change initiative relates to generating awareness, understanding and developing the new capabilities required to change amongst the target community – in this case, your team.

Communications

Awareness and understanding of the change are achieved through communication. Communication is such an important area of change that I have allocated the next chapter to focus on it specifically. I will make a few summary points now.

Communicating about change is not simply a matter of telling your team members about your change. If you want your team members to support the change, you need to carefully develop messages explaining why the change is being pursued, what the change is and how it will affect them personally. You cannot just tell these messages to people once and expect them to absorb them. Good communication about change requires regular consistent reinforcement of clear messages – messages which are ideally compelling to the target audience. Different members of your team may require different styles of communication. Finally, what you communicate as the leader of the team is at least as much about your behaviour as it is about the words you use.

Skills development and training

To be confident a change will work – and that team members can adapt to it – you must check that people have the skills and capabilities to perform in the new way. Your team members may need training, coaching, guidance or just some quick tips from you. This is dependent on the scale and novelty of the change you are undertaking. For more complex changes you should undertake a training needs assessment. A training needs assessment is a formal assessment of the training needs of a group. If you decide you do need to do this, you will probably need specialist help – start by asking your HR department for support.

The training needs assessment will provide you with an in-depth understanding of any skill or capability gaps, and you can then decide the most appropriate way to close the gap. You may not be able to do a full training needs assessment until some way through the lifecycle of the change initiative, when the details of the change and the impact on the affected community are fully understood. However, if the change is significant and has a separate budget, it is worth doing at least a rough-and-ready assessment at the start of the project. Then, if you need to invest in training you can try to build a budget for training into the change initiative's budget.

A need for new skills should not lead to the automatic conclusion that formal or external training is required. There are many ways of learning new skills. Sometimes training can be achieved by cross-training between peers in your team. You can choose to develop your own training materials for self-teaching as part of the change initiative. Some skills are best acquired as on-the-job learning once the change is implemented. Consider selecting one member of the team to become the subject-matter expert to guide and advise other team members.

Think this through thoroughly and consider the implications of which training is best. Often the form of skills development provided is less a function of need and more a function of available budgets. You will not always need formal training, and even when you do, you may not be able to afford it. But if it is required and you do not provide it, then you are adding risk to your change and to business-as-usual performance levels once the change is completed.

An often forgotten benefit of training is that many team members will appreciate being able to undertake training. It shows a willingness to invest, creates a sense that the individual team member is valued and helps to develop goodwill. None of these reasons will magically create money if you have none, but if you have the budget and are wavering as to whether to spend it or not, do not forget these important side benefits from training.

Training should be included within your change project plan. Other learning supports, such as providing guidance and quick tips, come from the way you react and respond to your team during periods of change. You must be responsive to individuals' differing speeds to learn and adopt change. When you are planning the change, think through how different the skills the team will require after the change will be from the skills required now. The bigger the variation, the more likely that team members will need training. The more training required, the more likely that it will have an impact on budgets.

Skills, recruitment and redundancy

Occasionally, when you perform your assessment of the skills needed to work in the new way you may come to a more difficult conclusion. You may realise that some people in your team do not have the skills required, and that the gap in capabilities is so large that it is practically unbridgeable. You should always be careful drawing these conclusions, and if you do, explore options for how you may bridge the gap. But it is likely that sometimes you will decide that as a result of a change you need to alter the membership of your team. There are different ways of doing this, such as moving the people without the requisite skills into another team. Unfortunately, a common outcome in this situation is redundancy.

If you come to this decision your first step should be to discuss this with your HR department and your line manager. You may subsequently need specialist HR legal advice. Formally, you do not make people redundant, but remove their roles. However, in many situations this is little more than a verbal nicety – when the role is made redundant the person loses their job.

brilliant tip

Redundancy versus sacking

As an aside, redundancy is *not* being sacked. An individual is sacked when they lose their job for performance or disciplinary issues. In the case of sacking the individual is at fault. On the other hand, redundancy is not a personal criticism. It is a result of an organisation no longer needing a role. The individual is not at fault in this situation. Sacking is something quite different. The reason I stress this is that it plays into the way you should deal with and communicate about redundancy and resulting job losses.

There are practical constraints on making people redundant (e.g. budgets for redundancy pay), as well as legal constraints (i.e. having a legally valid justification). There are ways you may legitimately make team members redundant, and there are ways and reasons you may not. Find yourself attempting to make people redundant when you do not have the right or have not followed the right process, and you risk being on a fast track to an industrial tribunal. The precise rules applicable depend on national law and employment regulations. If your team is an international team you will have to deal with different laws in different countries. This can create complex and varying assessments of suitability, supporting data collection and logistics which should be planned in detailed. Specialist advice is essential.

A good starting point is to deliberate on the points in chapter 2. Have you done the management basics? These can provide essential support to any valid grounds you have for selecting who to make redundant. You also need to think about the impact on the rest of your team – redundancy does not just affect the person losing their job.

Redundancy is a reality of the modern world. It should not be treated lightly.

Fortunately, change is not merely associated with redundancy. It is often accompanied by recruitment. Change initiatives can result in a growth of the team and a need for additional staff. Change initiatives can also result in the need for new skills which result in new hires being brought on.

Recruitment is something all managers have to do periodically. It never seems to go as smoothly or quickly as expected! It is outside the scope of this book to discuss recruitment in detail, but some key factors for team leaders to consider include:

- **Budget and headcount:** to undertake recruitment you need to have the budget for the new staff as well as the approval for the headcount in your team. Care is especially required when recruitment spreads over budget years. Budgets and headcount levels have a habit of being altered across budget years. A separate budgetary issue to think through is the fact that the recruitment process can result in costs on top of direct staff salary costs.

- **Internal versus external recruitment:** one important consideration is whether you are seeking a recruit externally to your organisation or internally. Some organisations insist that all new roles are offered internally first. This needs to be factored into your expected timescales for recruitment. Particular care should be taken during the obviously sensitive situations in which your organisation is simultaneously making roles redundant and recruiting. Sometimes staff who held roles which are being made redundant have specific rights to the first opportunity to apply for any new roles.

- **Temporary versus permanent headcount:** are the new roles permanent headcount, or a temporary role on a short-term contract?

- *Specific role needs:* there are lots of factors about the specific role including the obvious factors like qualifications and experience, but also less obvious ones such as whether the role can be done part-time, working from home and so on.

There are many factors to be considered and taken into account when planning for recruitment. Economic conditions can make a huge difference. My experience is that it is possible to recruit relatively quickly, but recruitment for a variety of reasons tends to be a long-drawn-out process. The right candidate can be hard to find. When there are multiple positions to fill, this tendency for elongated duration of recruitment increases. Be realistic when it comes to recruitment: how long will it really take in your organisation? What you will do in the interim before the new people are on board?

Willingness to change: gaining support, reducing resistance

The willingness to adopt change is something you can try to predict. If you know your team well, your prediction will give you some idea of the range of responses you will have to deal with. It is generally obvious if a change is largely to the benefit or detriment of your team members – and from this it is not hard to conclude the likely responses. In practice, this will give you at best rough guidance. Individuals' reactions to change are often surprising.

I have had to prepare for tense meetings in which I have been involved in sharing bad news with teams about job losses or changes to terms and conditions – and found myself having open, friendly conversations about how to make the best of things. I have walked into meetings talking about what I perceived to be trivial or even beneficial changes, only to find myself dealing with a highly emotive and hostile reception. The point about willingness to change is that it needs to be assessed from the viewpoint of the affected party. Unless you know someone well and also know the other pressures and factors happening in their life, you will not be able to predict their response with any certainty.

> willingness to change needs to be assessed from the viewpoint of the affected party

Resistance

Willingness is one of the possible reactions to change. However, the more common and normal human reaction to change is resistance. There are many reasons why people resist changes. A few common examples are:

- The fact that as human beings we naturally thrive in conditions of stability which change disrupts. I know some people claim they love change. They normally mean they love change on their terms. It won't always be on their terms.

- When you ask someone to do something in a new or different way it can be perceived as a threat or a criticism of the previous ways they have worked. Some individuals can be very sensitive to this.

- Individuals may like the current ways of working, and a change can create a sense of loss.

- Change may be seen as risking someone's entitlements or benefits or simply making their life a bit harder.

- Resistance may be based on team members' concerns about the practicality of the proposed changes – and these concerns may be perfectly valid and well thought through. It is always worth listening to people's concerns about change. Some of the concerns will be unsubstantiated, but others will point to real issues that you should deal with.

- Resistance may be based on a feeling of unfairness, that the change applies to one group but not another, or because there is a perceived mismatch between the description of the change and the behaviour of the organisation's senior management or leadership. (Human beings are brilliant observers of behaviour and inconsistencies in it, and have perfect antennae for unfairness!)

- Resistance may be based on a belief that a change breaches previous promises made to team members. Be careful with making unconditional promises to team members. Organisational situations change and there is significant risk you may not be able to keep unconditional commitments forever.

- Some individuals resent having to learn new skills. This may be laziness, but it can also be associated with fear of failure or fear of new skills being less enjoyable.

- Resistance can arise when teams are unused to changing. Change seems to be easier to pursue, with less resistance, in organisations in which change is a common occurrence.

These reactions to change will not always be based on fact. They are often based on perception and influenced by how much your team trusts you. It will be significantly influenced by the team's past experience of changes. Frequently, resistance is not a fully rational reaction, but is an instinctive or emotional response. That does not alter the fact you need to deal with it. Understanding the variety of reasons for resisting change is important because when you understand this, you will be better positioned to manage such resistance and can avoid many of the traps managers commonly fall into.

Part of your change approach must be how you deal with any resistance to change you find. In an ideal world you would aim to remove any resistance. This is often not practical, at least not in the short run. Reflect back on Lewin's field force diagram. Your aim at a minimum must be to try and ensure that the promoting forces are greater than the resisting forces. When you start out on a change initiative, the resistance may be the stronger force. By a combination of good argument, appeals, education, modification of your changes, concession, rewards for conformance and occasional use of penalties you must seek to overcome the resistance to a sufficient degree to achieve your change outcomes.

Resistance is natural. If you have limited patience or a short temper, take a deep breath and stay calm. There is no point getting angry about it. It is just something you have to deal with in progressing change. In the rest of this section, I look at some simple tools to understand and overcome resistance, as well as typical situations you have to learn to resolve.

The balance between support and resistance is not only a factor of what a change is. It is significantly affected by how a change is explained and managed.

The change curve

Earlier in this chapter I introduced one change management model or tool, Lewin's field force analysis. Now I want to introduce one of the classic pieces of change management thinking – the change curve. There are many versions of this, but all originate in the work and writings of Elisabeth Kübler-Ross. The change curve explains the stages people go through in adapting from one way to a new way.

The change curve represents proven and known stages everyone goes through when experiencing change. The important point is that you cannot miss out stages in the change curve – but you can go through them faster or slower depending on the change, your personality, the context and the support you receive from those around you.

Kübler-Ross's ideas are encapsulated in her five stages of grief model. While they originate in her work researching how people deal with death and dying, you should not think about it as morbid. The thinking is fully transferable to other change situations. The five stages she identified are: denial, anger, bargaining, depression and acceptance. Her model has been enhanced by other researchers in change, and sometimes slightly different names are used for the stages, but the principles remain the same. Some change management professionals can be quite pedantic about the stages in the change curve. For me, the precise names for the stages and the number of stages is less relevant than developing an awareness of the overall shape of how people accept change (see Figure 7.3).

The change curve is useful for you to understand your own state in the change, and to understand others' states and help them through it. It provides a language which you can use to talk about change, and become self-aware of your own mental state. This self-awareness is very helpful, as it shows that feelings about change are perfectly normal. Your aim in managing change is to make sure people flow easily through all the stages in the change curve, not getting stuck at any stage and not taking forever to pass through it.

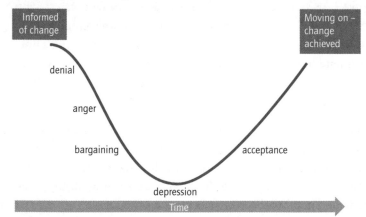

Figure 7.3 Change curve
Source: Kubler-Ross, *On Death and Dying, Routledge, 1969*

As part of change initiatives it can be useful to educate members of your team in field force analysis and the change curve. They are conceptually simple but powerful, and if you will repeatedly embark on change they provide some good reusable tools. They also help people to understand and cope with their own responses to change.

Explaining change (communications again!)

Your main tool for convincing people to support a change is what you say. Great communications are a significant factor in developing strong support and reduced resistance for many changes. We are going to look at communications in detail in chapter 8, and I don't want to have an extensive discussion here. But there are some specific points to bear in mind when contemplating willingness to change and encouraging change adoption.

When you are preparing to introduce a change to your team, start by thinking through exactly what you are going to say and how you say it. Many elements of resistance come from misunderstanding what the change is. If you are not clear, or alter your messages, your team will not understand the change. People who don't understand are more likely to resist.

While you will almost certainly start by explaining the general reasons for a change and why your organisation wants to pursue it, when you introduce the change to your team you are talking to individuals. They may care deeply and passionately about the organisation as a whole, or they may be indifferent. They will certainly want to understand what the change means for them. In providing this information team members will appreciate it if you come across as really talking to them and not just regurgitating some corporate messages.

If you have communicated change often, you will know that people have a fantastic ability to misinterpret what you mean – generally making your life difficult. To avoid this you need to be willing not only to talk about the change, but to listen to responses. If responses come from a misinterpretation of what you meant, take the time to explain and explain again until the misinterpretation has been resolved.

Try to avoid too much management jargon and use simple everyday words. Lots of jargon makes people feel you are not talking to them personally.

Mental models, fixed assumptions and default thinking

One of the most difficult parts of change to deal with is when change challenges deeply held beliefs. Often these beliefs are only partially conscious but are built into the underlying assumptions with which people view the world. They may exist as mental models and how activities and the culture at work are understood. They may also be reflected by a tendency to revert to default and unreflective thinking. Having assumptions, mental models and a reliance on unquestioned default thinking are normal parts of everyone's mental life.

An example of an assumption affecting change is the situation in which an organisation relocates a major office to another town but the affected team have always assumed the organisation is part of that community. While the change is not challenging any explicit aspects or stated aims of the organisation, it is challenging a valued and deeply held belief.

The problem with hidden assumptions is that you cannot develop compelling counter arguments to beliefs and assumptions you are unaware of. If you find and challenge such beliefs, you can find yourself facing a strong emotional response.

There are two ways of dealing with such fixed assumptions. The first is to try and expose them, so they can be discussed. This usually takes time, and requires empathetic questioning of your team members until they are exposed. Sometimes one of the barriers to doing this is you, as you may share the same assumptions. The second way is to generally raise awareness of your team to the idea that we have assumptions, mental models and default thinking. This requires discussion and sometimes training to understand how we constrain ourselves by the models and unquestioned assumptions we have.

There is not an easy answer to resolving issues with unspoken assumptions. But if your change challenges them and you do not invest the time in trying to deal with them, you will face extended resistance to the change.

What if the change is bad news?

Many change management advisors, books and courses present change as if it is something wonderful. Resistance is natural, but is explained as an erroneous response that you can put right. The truth is more complex. Change may be great news for the organisation as a whole, while being bad news for specific individuals in your team. In this situation you are unlikely to gain support for a change. The best you can do is to moderate the resistance.

The challenge with a change which really is bad news is to balance fair and ethical interactions with your team with the desire to avoid negative impacts on your team's performance. You have to mull over what the best timing is. In general terms, I always advise people to be as open as possible as soon as possible. In doing this, you need to be ready to deal with the inevitable negative response. You also need to be clear about how team members are going to be treated as they go through the change. A common reaction from team members is to try to bargain.

Bargaining

One response to change is bargaining. It seems an automatic response ingrained from childhood – *you are asking me to do X, I don't want to do X, but I will do X if you give me something in return.* Whether you are prepared to bargain, and what in practice you have to offer, needs to be decided in advance of starting on your change journey. Otherwise you will end up bargaining on the fly, which is rarely a good approach.

If you are expecting team members to do something significantly different as a result of a change – and in some way this is detrimental to them – then it is not unreasonable for them to expect something in return. Sometimes bargaining becomes a formalised group response to a change. This is a common situation if you work in a unionised organisation.

Bargaining is a big subject, and I cannot cover it fully here. But I can offer a few key points, relevant to the team manager and team change.

- Be alert to what you are saying to team members. It is easy to accidentally start bargaining. Once you do it is hard to revert back from bargaining without making the change even harder.

- If you do decide to bargain, money is not your only bargaining chip. There are lots of things that are of value to your team members, which they may be willing to take in order to accept an unpopular change. For example, the ability to work at home one day a week is something many people value highly.

- Do not give rewards just for changing. This sets a very bad precedent and may result in a sense of entitlement that a reward will be given for every change. You will also make yourself unpopular with your peers trying to pursue their own team changes. Change is a normal part of a modern job, and team members should expect to adapt to reasonable change without reward.

- If there are absolute givens about the change then make them clear. There is no point opening up discussions about elements of the change which are non-negotiable. You will only create trouble for yourself!

- If it is only a small number of your team members who are trying to negotiate, then be careful offering anything – otherwise soon your whole team will start asking for something.

- Consider the knock-on impact of anything you agree to as part of bargaining. For example, if you agree to change terms and conditions for some staff, how will this be perceived by the rest of the team – and by staff in other teams? You may be tempted to try and secretly negotiate with some team members and not others. Such secrets rarely stay secret.

- If bargaining is a serious likelihood you should seek both permission and help. If you think you have to make a concession, is it within your authority to give it? Are you capable of doing this sort of negotiation? If not, don't try to be a hero, seek help. Sources of help include HR and your boss.

- Think long term about concessions. This cuts both ways. Some concessions are worth it for better, positive team relationships and swift change. However, other concessions may cause you problems months or even years later.

Try to avoid getting into a bargaining situation if you can. I am not saying that you shouldn't be fair. If you need to reward or recompense staff for some aspect of the change, design it in and make this offer as part of the change. But sometimes, especially for very significant and contentious change, some level of negotiating will arise and you should prepare for it.

Your personal change journey and becoming the change leader

The change curve is a useful tool in helping your team. It is also a useful tool in helping yourself to understand your own feelings about the change. As a team leader you may be the originator of

change, but often change comes from outside the team. You can feel as much a victim of the change as any other member of your team. The change may directly affect the way you work, your role and other elements of your daily life within the organisation. You need to adapt to the change as well. In this case you will take your own journey through the change curve. This may be as intense, as demanding and as emotional as it is for any other member of your team.

It is worth highlighting the need for you as a manager to act as a role model for the change – making sure your behaviour is aligned to the goals of the change. This may be in conflict with your own feelings. But if you do not show support then the change will struggle, or it will not happen. People are more likely to follow what you do than what you say. This is the core of leading change – setting an example for your team, showing that

> people are more likely to follow what you do than what you say

the change works and making sure that all of your behaviour is consistent with your talk about the change. You need to role model the change. Why should anyone else follow if you won't yourself?

Part of the change leadership is taking time to engage with and communicate to your team members as individuals and as a group. Communication is very important, and your team members will listen to your words. But even more, they will observe your behaviour. People are quick to identify discrepancies between someone's words and behaviour. If your team notice this in you, they will regard you as a hypocrite. The most successful leaders walk the talk. This is the ethical thing to do. It is also a much more effective way to guide change.

As you undertake change in your team that personally affects you, you may find yourself developing a higher than usual level of stress. You may also be at times confused about what is the

most appropriate course of action to take as a change throws up problems. It can be helpful for you to find someone to support you, talk to and advise you on the change. This may be your line manager, but often the nature of the conversations is such that you may feel you cannot discuss things openly with your boss because you do not have the right relationship with him. In these situations, it is helpful to have a more experienced peer or senior manager who is not your boss to go to for advice – acting as a change mentor. Having such a mentor will improve your own endurance during change, and provide you with a source of additional wisdom.

Team change

So far in this chapter we have discussed change from the perspective of the individual – be it a member of the team or you as the team leader. But you do not just lead a group of individuals, you lead a team. The members of your team interact and have an influence on each other. In normal business-as-usual work, ideally the performance of the team is greater than the performance would be if the individuals worked separately. The goal of most teams is for the sum to be greater than the parts.

In a change situation you must reflect not only on individuals, but also on the team as a whole. There are two aspects to this you should ponder, observe and take appropriate action to deal with. The first aspect is related to working through the change: how the behaviour of the team affects individuals' willingness to change. The second is related to the outcome or results from the change: how the change affects the performance of your team as a team.

Behaviour of the team

We are all liable to be influenced by the people around us. Teams tend to subject team members to all sorts of peer pressures and expectations about norms of behaviour in the team. This is not a bad thing – in fact it is something most team leaders welcome in many situations. A largely productive and well-functioning team tends to pull other people along into being productive and effective employees. You want your team to have a strong bond in which they help each other, and this leads to people creating supportive coalitions within the team.

But team culture can become destructive as well as constructive. Change can be the impetus for unhelpful behaviour. Rather than seeing itself as part of the wider organisation, a team can become a unit which sees itself as trying to survive in spite of the actions of management or the wider organisation. Team bonds may be stronger than team member–manager, or team member–organis-ation bonds. What is a powerful aid to productivity in normal situations can convert into a battle during change. Rather than trying to help individuals through change, you may in effect find yourself having to attempt some form of collective bargaining.

You must try to predict, monitor and react to the response of the team as a unit as well as the individuals in it. There are numerous strategies for managing teams through change. One useful approach is to identify the key opinion formers in the team and work with them to gain support for the change. Often there are individuals, not necessarily in positions of formal power, who have greater influence on the team's attitude to change than others.

> identify the key opinion formers in the team and work with them to gain support for the change

If you are a unionised organisation any significant change will require interacting with union representatives using the agreed channels. If you are unfamiliar with the approach to working with unions it is worth seeking out advice from other managers in the organisation. Large organisations often have a dedicated manager or team responsible for union relationships. With well-established union relationships there are often defined formal ways of communicating and negotiating about change. If you have constructive union relationships, there are also often ways of discussing and testing ideas with union representatives informally prior to moving into implementation. These are worth using as they can help shape changes and your approach to implementing them.

Your team is not a homogeneous unit. When you are planning change and thinking about how to deal with issues, consider two specific groups. First, there are usually key influencers: individuals who have a disproportionate effect on the overall mood and attitude of the team. Secondly, there are your key staff: individuals who either do a disproportionate percentage of the work of your team or have some rare critical skills. You should pay particular attention to these two types of individuals through change.

Impact of the change on the team

Change will often have an impact on the effectiveness of the team as a unit. There are obvious situations such as when you recruit new people in new roles into the team, or when roles are eliminated from the team when the dynamics of the team alter. But even when the people in the team stay the same there are many situations that will reduce the effectiveness of the team – for example, if roles are altered or if individuals start to work with people they have not worked with closely before.

A team operates at a certain level of performance. There are normal fluctuations in this performance, but we are all aware of well running and poorly performing teams. These performance levels are a result of a complex set of factors, including the way you interact and manage the team, as well as the team's level of maturity and familiarity with each other.

One of the best ways of thinking about this derives from Bruce Tuckman's 1965 model of group development. This model was contained in his paper 'Developmental Sequence in Small Groups'. This model has become a common reference point for management and leadership discussions and is widely referred to in academic and non-academic writing. It is most famous for the four stages of team development Tuckman identified of forming, norming, storming and performing. These names of these stages have become everyday parts of many managers' vocabulary.

Tuckman argued that these stages are all necessary and inevitable in the development of a team. A team must go through all four stages to reach the performing stage. Some teams make this passage more easily than others, and some teams become dysfunctional or underdeveloped by getting stuck at an earlier stage. Tuckman argued not all teams will get to the performing stage.

What change managers have realised is that change disrupts a team, and a team which was at the performing stage, operating as a mature and effective team, can be pushed back to an earlier stage. Very significant change will push a team back to the forming stage. Even relatively modest change can temporarily move a team out of the performing stage.

This has implications for business-as-usual productivity and quality of work. It also has implications for you as a manager. You may start a change with a mature team, and end it with an immature team you need to help to achieve maturity again. It is often helpful and even necessary to plan some specific team-building activities following a significant change.

> you may start a change with a mature team, and end it with an immature team

Building and maintaining belief in the change

One key facet of any change initiative it is important to think through is how to develop people's faith or belief in the success of the change project. If your change project is short – taking days, weeks or a couple of months – then you do not need to worry about this. But some changes take many months or even years to implement. It is important to keep individuals supporting the change over long periods. Support is most likely when people believe your change will be successful. It's hard to keep such belief for months and years without a reason.

There are several ways to generate and maintain such faith. One factor is your behaviour and language and that of other influential line managers or executives your team interacts with. Try to keep the tone of language positive and focussed on the outcome. This can be hard, with very long-duration change initiatives, especially in face of the inevitable problems that will occur now and again. If you are ever starting to doubt or lose faith in the change, try not to express this or indicate it to your team. Try also to influence other managers to keep a positive view of the change.

Another way of building and maintaining belief is by the use of examples. Try to find case studies of other teams or organisations that have done something similar successfully. Even better if you can take your team members to visit such a team. People who have implemented change successfully are usually happy to share the story of their successes with you. If you do this, it is a good way to learn any pitfalls you might reach and how to avoid them. It is also a good way of making people understand that any short-term pain is worth it for the longer-term benefit.

One of the strongest ways of developing faith is by creating intermediate tangible progress on a change initiative. A good way to do this is with quick wins. Quick wins are small but visible improvements you achieve during your change project. The win may not be terribly important in itself, but if it is visible it gives people a reason to believe in your change project – and to maintain their support. Such quick wins should be designed into your change initiative plan.

brilliant recap

At the heart of change management is the process of helping individuals adapt to and adopt the desired change. As part of the change initiative you must find a way to ensure that individuals in the team will have:

● An awareness that a change is occurring.

● An understanding of the change and its implications for them.

● The capability and skills to work in the way the change requires.

● A willingness to work in the new way.

On top of this, the working environment must be such that the reasons to adopt the change are stronger than those opposing it. One way of visualising this is via Lewin's field force diagram.

This leads to various activities including communications, education and sometimes formal training. Change initiatives can also result in alterations to the people in your team through recruitment, redundancy or both. On top of the purely practical aspects of awareness and understanding of a change, and capability to conform to the change, is the human issue of willingness to change.

Willingness to change is counterbalanced by human beings' tendency to resist change. This is an individual issue and people's responses to change vary hugely.

In some situations you will find yourself bargaining over the change. If this is likely, prepare in advance.

A good way to understand the process we all go through in change is the change curve. Remember that often this applies as much to you as the team leader as it does the team members.

As a team leader you are not simply managing a group of individuals. You are managing a team. The team as a unit has an impact on the change adoption. First in the way that factors such as peer behaviour and peer pressure influence adoption of the change. Secondly, how change affects the working of a team. One way of thinking about this is with Tuckman's model of group development. A team may need some help rebuilding once a significant change is complete.

It is important for the successful adaptation to and adoption of change to build and maintain belief about the change. A useful approach is to find a regular stream of quick wins for the duration of the change initiative.

CHAPTER 8

Talking about change

A common complaint at work is the lack of communication. This is expressed whenever team members are asked what their biggest challenges are. People from across organisations bemoan the lack of effective communication. Yet many senior managers put significant effort into communicating. You will often hear their complaint that they are doing so many presentations, attending so many town halls and team meetings, or doing so many one-to-ones with team members that they have no time to get on with other aspects of their job.

Communication is a central task of managers in all organisations. In times of change communication becomes even more important and more intense. Somehow communication seems to be a constant point of frustration for both the recipients of information and the people doing the communicating. Something is wrong.

I think there are some common contributors to this issue. Much of the problem is down to a lack of structured thinking about communications. This should start with a clear understanding of why you are communicating, who you are communicating with, and what are the most appropriate and compelling messages for that audience. Perhaps because talking comes so naturally to us, we do not think about it enough. Often we just talk instead of thinking first.

Another problem is that many people undervalue their role as communicators. Whenever I hear a manager complaining about

the tool for interaction is communication

the amount of time they spend in meetings or giving presentations, I ask: *what do you think your job is, if not communicating?* Management is inherently concerned with interaction. The tool for interaction is communication.

Whenever you hear someone complaining about communication, try to analyse what the problem really is. When people say there is not enough communication at work they rarely literally mean it. What they normally mean is there is not enough communication of the right sort.

In this chapter I assume you are a typical team leader in a typical organisation. You do not have the support of a dedicated communication professional. On a large change programme you may have access to, and may need, a communication team – but let's take that as a bonus rather than the situation you will normally find yourself in. I will try to set your expectations about quite how much communication a change initiative requires, how to think about and prepare communications and how to provide the *right sort* of communication.

There is a very rough logical ordering to most of the chapters in this book. This chapter is an exception. Communication is not something that happens at a specific phase of your change initiative. Your communication should be like a drum beat that sounds throughout the life of your initiative. As such, this chapter could be positioned anywhere in the book. Just because you find it at chapter 8, don't think communications starts towards the end of your initiative!

Change and communication

There are many reasons to communicate during a change programme, which can be summarised into a few main categories:

- **Passing information:** that is, transmitting of facts and supporting messages about the change initiative. This will include general information about why it is being done, updates on progress and answers to questions. Such information may be general or targeted at a specific audience.

- **Collecting information:** this may be purely factual and quantitative information, such as progress towards completion of tasks or performance metrics. It is often more qualitative information such as understanding your team members' concerns and issues, and understanding their mood.

- **As a vehicle of change:** communications can be used to influence behaviour and garner support for the change. We have all experienced someone 'talking up' a change. A good argument may increase support and overcome doubts about a change. Communication alone won't deliver sustained change, but it can start the process going and is a key part of most changes.

- **Governance:** governance relates to the decision-making processes surrounding a change. You will need to communicate to gain approvals and get the decisions made.

These are all sensible and practical reasons to communicate. Communication is also important as a way of influencing the mood and levels of trust of the affected members of your team. Often in a change situation trust takes a hit. It's easy for people to become worried and suspicious. Change can create a sense among your team that decisions are being made behind their backs about them, about their jobs and about the activities they do. This may be true, but it is easy to get overly mistrustful. Rarely is the truth worse than the imagination. Team members who are worried about change and distrustful of their managers are unlikely to be fully engaged in work.

One way of moderating these feelings is with appropriate communication. It's important to be sensitive and responsive to team members' mood on change initiatives. In reality, you cannot always tell people everything they want to know. Sometimes change initiatives will mean bad news for your team. But careful communication can at least moderate the worst effects of stress, mistrust and a hunger for information.

Common communication challenge 1: secrecy versus openness

The ability to communicate is obviously partially determined by your communication skills. On top of this, managers often struggle with two specific issues during change. One is openness – relating to concerns about sharing sensitive information about the change. The second is timeliness – that is, the ability to provide information in a timely manner. These issues are discussed on almost every significant change initiative I have been involved with. Let's look at each of these issues.

It's usually much easier and better to be open than people think. Of course, there are some things that must remain confidential and which can only be announced at certain times or when certain decisions have been made. These are normally a relatively limited number of situations in the programme.

What should you do if you think the change should be a secret? You are probably worrying because the change touches on sensitive issues such as redundancy or alterations in benefits. First, ask yourself if you really can keep it secret. Most organisations I have worked in are much worse at keeping secrets than they would like to think they are. I think it is better that you are open with bad news than let it leak out. Leaks fuel cynicism and mistrust. Second, ask yourself what you are trying to achieve by keeping it secret. Usually, you are trying to avoid giving staff de-motivational news that might detrimentally affect business-as-usual performance. Are you stopping a blip in performance, or merely making the blip happen at a different time? If the blip will happen anyway, it may be better to get it over and done with.

You may not be worried about a temporary but rather an extended drop in performance. Then there is more of an incentive for secrecy. But keeping a change secret is not the only way to avoid this problem. You may, for example, seek ways to motivate or reward team members for maintaining high performance in the face of information about a change they respond to badly. However, this is not always appropriate or possible. If you really believe you should keep your intentions secret for a while, then do. But you have to be vigilant to stop leaks – otherwise the drop in performance will happen anyway.

Just keeping secrets to avoid difficult conversations is a poor reason for secrecy. You are only delaying the conversation. This is usually more stressful than getting it over and done with by being open at the outset of a change.

Another way of looking at this is to ask yourself what will happen if you do not communicate openly. Simple: it will happen anyway! Or at least

human beings are alert for communication

something will be communicated, but probably not what you want. The way you behave and what you don't talk about communicate as much as what you choose to talk about. You communicate all the time deliberately and accidentally. Human beings are alert for communication. When it does not come, they fill the gap with interpretation and supposition. There is no better way of getting the rumour mill going at work than for managers to start rushing off and huddling in rooms. This happens frequently on change initiatives when secrets are in the air.

A final thought on secrecy – the more often you keep secrets which are later exposed, the more you will be perceived as a manager who has secrets. If you want your team to trust you, be open.

Common communication challenge 2: timeliness and delays

The second common issue is communicating late. The importance of communication is often stressed to such an extent that people worry about perfecting and honing their communications to the nth degree. This results in communications being delayed as more information is collected and presentations are perfected. There are times when communications need to be perfect, but they are limited. I always stress the importance of good communication. But more important than any individual communication is building a stream of communication so there is little opportunity for a vacuum to be created, and rumour and gossip to fill the space. Think about ongoing flow of information more than individual presentations.

Occasionally, communication will have to be delayed because a change initiative has not progressed as quickly as expected, or some unanticipated problem has arisen. If something goes wrong, most often the best response is to put up your hand and say something has gone wrong and this will delay communication.

Remember you do not have to tell everyone everything at once. Tell your team members that you cannot tell them everything, because the initiative is still being worked out. This is better than silence. Set their expectations as to when you will be able to tell them. 'At time x we will be able to share this' or 'Once we know the results from... We will be able to update you'.

Don't let gaps in the information you have stop you communicating. Don't wait until you have the perfect speech or slide deck. Don't even try to hide the gaps in what you know. Yes, there is a minimum amount of information that makes it worth communicating, and below which you will not appear credible. But don't delay just because you cannot communicate everything you think you need to. Admit there are gaps. Then say that you will answer them later when the details are worked out. Some people will moan about this, but it is better than keeping them in the dark. (Some people will moan whatever you do!)

Best of all is to lay out a plan of when you will be able to tell people what they want to know. This, of course, requires you to have a good overall plan for the change.

How much communication is enough?

My basic rule of thumb for communication on a change initiative of any scale is to communicate much more than you think you need to. In my view, you cannot communicate too much during a change project. Your team and other stakeholders want to know why you are changing, what is changing, how the change is managed, how the change will affect the team. They want questions answered, progress to be clear and to be regularly updated. Through the process of communication they want to feel valued and respected.

The actual amount of communication required depends on the scale and complexity of the change. It should take account of the need to repeat and reinforce messages before they sink in. The only way to assess properly how much communication is required is to plan it out. But during change, if you ever feel you have communicated enough, assume you are wrong!

It's a two-way process!

Communication is a two-way process. Good communication is as much concerned with listening as transmitting. There is a host of information you will require as the change progresses. This includes getting a sense of your team's mood and response to the change. You will want to monitor how that response evolves as the change progresses. On top of this there is more straightforward information, such as whether certain tasks have been completed, and whether any practical problems are occurring as the change is implemented. You will not gain any of this without a willingness to observe and listen.

You need to listen because you need to gather information and understand the situation. Listening helps to develop the right relationships. You are also more likely to be listened to if you are perceived to be a good listener. Taking the time to listen to your team and being seen to do this are key aspects of building a strong relationship with your team.

Using listening as a way to build rapport is very effective. It requires that you not only listen, but that you are *seen to be listening*. An added advantage is that individuals who are perceived to listen well often get told things that poor listeners are not.

How to communicate: the elements of successful change communication

Now I want to explore how to communicate. I do this by explaining the elements that go into successful communications.

Goals

Communication is a goal-directed activity. In our everyday conversations we do not consciously think in terms of our goals. When planning communication on a change initiative, before you say or write anything, think through why you need to communicate. It may be to transmit information, influence people's opinion, get specific actions undertaken and so on. This may seem obvious, but much management communication is muddled and

> before you say or write anything, think through why you need to communicate

ineffective. Often the communicator has not thought through why they are communicating, and has not designed the communication for that goal.

Start by asking yourself why you need to communicate. Until you can answer this question, you won't produce effective communications, except by luck.

Audiences

The next point to think through is who is the audience for your communication? Who needs to know what, who needs to be engaged and influenced to make this change a success? In chapter 5 we looked at identifying and managing stakeholders. All of your communication is related to engaging and influencing stakeholders. But you need different things from different stakeholders, therefore they need to be influenced by different messages and styles of communication.

One important question is which stakeholders can you group together as needing similar messages presented in a similar way, and who has to be treated separately? The most effective communication is a tailored one-to-one engagement. The most efficient is blanket standard communication to all. You must find the right balance between the two, weighing up pragmatism against perfection.

I am always reminded of the old newspaper saying – 'there is no news but local news'. Our idea of what is local may be different from in the past, but the sentiment still holds. Group people together if the same sorts of communications are relevant and effective to them; separate them if they are not.

Include considerations of terminology in your assessment of grouping. If your team is specialised, it will usually have its own specialist terminology and jargon. This might not be the language that stakeholders use, and may mean nothing to them.

The words you choose have to be appropriate, meaningful and compelling to the audience you are talking to.

Messages

What sort of things should you communicate about? The precise things you need to communicate will vary from situation to situation, but in general terms you should consider communicating regularly. The foundations of good communication are good messages – messages which are relevant and clear as well as compelling for the audiences they are targeted at.

There are some common questions you will have to answer on any change initiative:

- *Why does the change need to happen?* You need to describe the context and objectives, and justify the change.
- *Why does it need to happen now?* You should explain the urgency for the change.
- *What is the change?* You must clearly describe the goals of the change initiative.
- *How will the change be pursued?* You need to show the plan and the approach.
- *What do you want individuals to do, and how do you want them to behave?* You should explain how individuals can constructively contribute to the change.
- *How will the change affect each individual?* You should seek to make the change relevant to each team member.

Start by thinking about messages, not media. The horrible tendency for modern managers to leap straight to PowerPoint should be resisted. I am not an enemy of PowerPoint. I use it a lot. Used *appropriately* it is a great tool. But it is not appropriate for many uses. I do not believe it is a good tool for thinking through messages in the first place. It is a helpful tool for presenting them once you have developed them.

If you are stuck for something to say, but feel there is a need for information or updates on the change, use the plan as part of communication. When there is nothing else to communicate, the plan itself is interesting to many audiences. It will show when different activities and outcomes are expected, and when more informative communications will be ready.

Channels

There are many different channels of communication, and an increasing proliferation of those channels: direct conversations, emails, town halls, presentations, meetings, internal social media, newsletters and text messages. Each of these channels has strengths and weaknesses, and may be appropriate for certain communications. A classic example is email, which is great for the easy mass communication of uncontentious information but is a terrible way to develop rapport or to sensitively share difficult messages.

Some communication channels are easy for targeting large numbers of people. Others are more intimate. While you may want your communications to be efficient, intimacy counts for a lot and is essential for building rapport and trust. You will have to use formal communication channels at times – fixed meetings, emails, periodic newsletters and the like. These can be helpful, but don't rely only on the formal communication channels. They are rarely sufficient, timely or responsive enough. Try to walk the floor and find other ways for informal conversations. You will learn a lot this way.

It is unusual in an organisational change programme to use external social media, but if you do you should take care about what you share. Once it's out there, you can't pull it back!

The best way is to use a range of media. Apply common sense. If you struggle to see why different media are more or less relevant, then take advice.

Reinforcement

Messages will not get through to all your stakeholders just because you say them once. The most effective and com-

the most effective and compelling messages may need to be repeated multiple times

pelling messages may need to be repeated multiple times. The process of reinforcement may occasionally be frustrating, but it is essential.

For messages to be effectively reinforced they must be consistent. It is surprising how often managers choose to alter their messages during a change. (I don't mean the precise set of words, I mean altering the underlying message those words convey.) This creates confusion and will not help your cause. It is another reason why it is worth getting your key messages right in the first place. Put another way, every time you change any of your key messages you are going backwards in achieving your communications goals and in making progress to your desired change.

Reinforcement is related to expectation setting. The communication you use is central to setting and maintaining expectations. If you want to set expectations and then deliver to these expectations you need consistent messages, and messages that have a strong correlation with reality.

Ten ground rules for communications

I want to end with some general ground rules about communication which summarise and build on many of these points. (These originally appeared in my book *Financial Times Briefing: Change Management*, see Table 8.1.)

Table 8.1 Communication ground rules

	Ground rule	Comment: relevance to change management
1.	Before you communicate anything, understand what you are trying to achieve.	Why are you communicating? If you cannot answer this question, you will never communicate coherently. The main reason so much management talk is incoherent is that the speakers do not understand clearly enough why they are talking. A vague feeling that 'I need to communicate' is not sufficient. If you are going to open your mouth it should be for a reason. Understand this reason and design your communication to fulfil it.
2.	Tailor communication to the audience.	Various groups respond to different language, formats, media, timing, etc. There is rarely a single audience and therefore there is rarely a single best form of communication. If you say the same thing in the same way to everyone, your communication will not be fully effective.
		There are many media formats and channels for communicating to stakeholders – do not become fixated on one or another (such as only using PowerPoint presentations). Adapt to the situation and the audience.
3.	Make communication as intimate and personally relevant as possible.	The less personally relevant the communication is to the audience, the less effective it tends to be. Of course, you cannot talk to every individual in a large organisation. Some things have to be emailed to everyone, but it is never as effective as a one-to-one interaction tailored to the individual. A balance must be found, and in general making the effort to find time to talk to and listen to smaller groups pays dividends.
4.	Regularly repeat your communications.	You will rarely be heard or fully understood the first time you say something, especially if the audience is large, the content is complex, or the message is contentious or unwelcome. Repetition works.
5.	Be consistent in what you say.	Repetition works best if you are consistent in what you say. Of course, messages evolve as initiatives progress, but if you are inconsistent you will cause confusion and lose trust. Perhaps worse for you personally, you will look incompetent.
		Consistency is a key factor in successful change. You should aim for consistency in messages, behaviour, rewards and policies, etc. Any inconsistency is confusing and gives reluctant members of staff a reason to delay changing.

	Ground rule	Comment: relevance to change management
6.	**Align your behaviour and actions with your words.**	Consistency is not just about saying the same thing again and again. You communicate far more than what you say. You communicate by what you are seen to do and how you do it. If your actions do not match your words people will notice – and it is your actions they will follow.
7.	**Don't communicate for the sake of it, but don't let a vacuum arise.**	You can waste time and effort on bad communication. People hate vacuous talk without substance. It wastes everyone's time. However, not talking at all can leave a vacuum which is filled with rumour and gossip. This is rarely helpful.
		If you really have nothing to say, tell people when you will have something to tell them. Talking about the process of communication that you will take people through as a change initiative unfolds is informative and helps inspire confidence.
		You must of course keep to any commitments you make!
8.	**Listen much more than you speak.**	Understanding comes from listening. Never forget that communication is a two-way process. Listening is particularly important in change initiatives. Listening enables you to gather information about resistance and ideas about the change. Your staff will have many great ideas. This includes improvements to the proposed change or the way it is being pursued. But listening does more than this – it also shows respect, builds relationships and trust. If people feel they are never listened to, they have a tendency to stop listening.
		The way you respond when you listen can encourage or inhibit essential upward communications. Take the attitude that any opinion is allowed, never 'shoot the messenger' and you will find out all sorts of useful information. If you constantly respond negatively to more junior staff's comments and questions you will soon find they stop speaking to you.
		Of the 10 rules on this list, this is the one many managers forget most often.

	Ground rule	Comment: relevance to change management
9.	Plan your communication.	Communication must not be ad hoc. It is too important to the success of your change initiative to be left to chance. As a critical activity it should be planned. If it is not, it will feel unprofessional and is likely to be inconsistent and insufficient. There are times you must be spontaneous, and having a plan should not stop this. Also, communication needs to evolve and the plan must evolve as well.
10.	Don't mistake talking for making progress.	Communication is an important tool. It is not the result.

What to communicate: the phases of a change initiative

The specific communications you will need to do and their timing will be unique to the change you are pursuing and the context in which you work. However, there are some fairly common stages all changes will go through from a communications perspective. There is the initial stage of explaining to people that a change is underway. There is the phase when the change initiative is ongoing when various updates need to be given, and usually dialogues kept going. There is the point in a change initiative when a change is actually implemented, when team members need to be prepared for the change. Finally, there is the close-down of the change initiative when you may need to keep listening to team members to ensure all is going well.

How you handle communicating at these stages depends on context and how open you have chosen to be. I always advise people to be as open as they can, and in this section I have assumed you are running an open change. Let's look at some communication tasks at each of these stages.

Breaking the news

The first element of communication to your team is to alert them to the fact that a change is being planned.

The initial messages can be fairly simple. *A change is occurring. We are pursuing it for the following reasons... It may affect you. We will keep you informed. For now, please keep focussed on the day job.*

Be ready to answer the obvious questions that will arise at this time. Mostly these will be of the form *why, why now, what, how* and *who is affected*. If you cannot answer these questions set a timeline of when you will be able to. There may be other questions that will obviously be asked in the context of the change you are about to pursue. Capture other questions and publish suitable answers – if appropriate as part of a set of frequently asked questions.

Set expectations of what it will be like during the process of change. *Work may become normally a bit less structured and occasionally chaotic as a change is executed. It may feel a little messy. This is normal, we are learning.* Present this as a normal factor of change and a situation in which learning happens. Set expectations about what you need people to do, and how you want them to behave as part of the change.

Keeping the conversation going

Once the change initiative is underway you will need to give regular updates to the team, and keep them engaged. This is best done by setting up a formal schedule of updates, and intermingling this with less formal chats around the office and casual conversations about the change.

This is the time when it is crucially important to listen as well as talk. The mood in a team can shift quickly if a change is not handled well or if it causes unexpected problems. You want to be quickly alerted to any operational difficulties the change creates so you can take appropriate action to deal with them.

It is usually worth developing an FAQ (frequently asked questions) list and publishing this so it is easily available. As questions arise you can maintain and extend this list. This reduces the need to answer the same question again and again.

Sometimes you will get difficult questions you cannot or do not want to answer yet – and you will get negative responses to the change from some of your team members. Don't think of those with difficult questions or negative views as the enemy. They are the people helping you to make the ideas more robust and who you must work with to take them on the change journey.

Implementing the change

A critical phase in your communication will occur when it comes to the time to implement the change. This depends on your implementation and transition plan. There might not be one big bang or there may be several. Or it may be a gradual transition to a new state.

Prior to implementation you must communicate to prepare people for any specific actions. Explain the transition and implementation plan. *What do you individually need to do? Will you have any training? Are there any other implications you need to be made aware of?* Explain how team members will be kept informed as the transition progresses.

Much of the communication during transition will relate to the mechanics of transitioning to the new way of working. But you need also to remind people about the need to remain vigilant and focussed on customer needs. This is also a good time to show your leadership skills and keep everyone motivated and in a positive mood.

After the change/bringing it to a close

It is always worth marking the end of a period of change. Talk to your team about letting the change settle down and fixing any residual problems. It is also a good point to reinforce that this is a permanent alteration in the way of working and there is no going back to the old ways. But this should not be done in a way that is seen as critical of the old ways – *they were right for their time and context, but now is a different time and context.*

This is also the appropriate time to give thanks for the support you have received during the change. Even if you do not feel like giving thanks and think you have had to push the change through in spite of ongoing opposition, there is little point bearing a grudge. Show your appreciation for the challenges you have given the team during the change, and try now to draw a line under them. If the change has been difficult then it can often be helpful to be explicit that it has been difficult. No one likes the insincerity of an overly positive thanks when everyone has hated the process and found it hard.

Following a change, you may be tempted to promise your team a period of stability. Don't do this unless you are certain it really will happen. Often the end of a change just signals the start of the next one. Although very significant change tends to be interspersed with periods of *relative* stability, how relative they are is a subjective and individual judgement.

When to communicate: planning communications

In the previous section I outlined some key stages of communication. For any significant change you should develop a communication plan. You can think of this as part of the overall change plan (as discussed in chapter 5), but normally the communication plan needs to be created as a separate document.

A simple way of developing a communication plan is to bring together two aspects of the change initiative. The first aspect is your stakeholders – that is, the different audiences you need to communicate to. The second aspect is the main activities and events on the change initiative plan. The thinking behind this is that the communication is to prepare different groups for what is happening on the change initiative. This can be presented as a matrix mapping one against the other. That can help trigger the thinking – *given what is happening in the change and who the stakeholders are, what needs to be communicated when?*

When I create a communications plan I start with a table sketched out on a flip-chart or white board. Down one side I put all the stakeholder groups and across the top I put the key events in the change initiative. I then correlate between each stakeholder group and each event on the change initiative. The first time this is done it can quickly become messy and complicated – a large white board is a good medium to work on.

The next thing to consider is the communications requirements implied by each intersection. When I think of a suitable communication activity I write it in the box that represents the intersection between a stakeholder group and an event. In some of the boxes there is no specific communication need as not every event needs to be communicated to every stakeholder group. But in many boxes you will decide on a suitable communication activity. This simple diagram is a powerful way to see what needs to be communicated when. An outline of such a table is shown in Table 8.2.

Table 8.2 Example of a table to assist with communications planning

Stakeholders	Key change initiative events					
	Event 1	Event 2	Event 3	Event 4	Event 5	Event 6
Stakeholder 1						
Stakeholder 2						
Stakeholder 3						
Stakeholder 4						

It's important to note that while the communications are done for major events on the programme, they may not be sequential with them. Some communication will happen before the event, some after. For example, say your change is going to result in you advertising 10 new roles to be recruited. When you think about this event you may decide that you want to communicate to your team about it several weeks in advance of the adverts being placed. You may wish to advise everyone when the adverts are published. Finally, you may need to communicate to people when the adverts will be removed. This is a simple example, but it should give you a sense of how to plan out your communications.

When you think through the communication plan, consider both the times you need to transmit and the times you need to listen. For some audiences you will need to produce regular updates on progress. But you also will need regular times to seek feedback from your team members, and other key stakeholders.

Logistics

Your communication plan builds from your identification of the points at which you need to communicate (either before, simultaneous to or following the key events on the change initiative). Add onto this any regular series of updates, progress reviews or listening sessions.

However, before you finalise your plan, consider your stakeholder's logistics. Some stakeholders, such as the members of your team, will more or less fit with whatever communication plan you have developed. But for some audiences, you must fit to their diaries and not the other way around. The classic example of this is a company's board. If you need to report your change at a board meeting, you had better plan those board meetings into your schedule. This is extreme; as a team leader you are unlikely to have to report directly to the board, but there may be other steering committees or groups that you will have to report to according to a fixed schedule.

Several change programmes I have been engaged in have run into major difficulties because people assumed they could communicate when they wanted to. In reality, for senior audiences you will have to communicate

> for senior audiences you will have to communicate when they want you to

when they want you to. This can lead to a situation in which the need to do certain communications can drive the pace of your overall change plan. The need to report to the board is the best example of this – but in your organisation there may be a host of boards, committees or already scheduled reviews which you need to align to. Make sure you work this out up-front when developing your plan.

Words versus other forms of communication

The importance of behaviour and the non-verbal aspects of our interaction with others is often commented on. Read any book or attend a course on communication skills and this will be stressed again and again. Ever since the famous experiments by Professor Albert Mehrabian in the 1960s, it has been understood that communication is not just about words. (If you don't know of these, they are worth reading up on.) Mehrabian's results are regularly quoted and usually misunderstood. But even though Mehrabian's results are often misinterpreted, there is no doubt that our communication is hugely affected by factors such as behaviour, facial expression, tone and speed of talking.

This is not a primer in communication skills, and it's way outside the scope of the book to teach you all the different aspects of communication. I have focussed in this section on verbal communication because I think it is important. Your behaviour and body language are critical to the way you build relationships and the responses you get to what you say. This does not mean that the words are not important.

The way I like to think of it is like this: your behaviour and body language will determine if people listen to you and to some extent if they believe what you say. People look and listen for congruence between what you say, how you say it and how you behave. We have well-developed antennae for determining if things don't match. Often we pick up inconsistencies, even though we cannot exactly put our finger on why we sense there is an inconsistency. If we sense such a discrepancy then we treat the words we hear as less credible. In extreme cases we do not even listen.

I have assumed in this section you know how to behave so that people will listen to you. Once people start to listen, then you need to worry about the words you use. If you cannot get people to listen to you, or people tend not to believe you, then you need to do something about this. A good place to start is by getting some feedback on your interaction style and behaviour. If it is a really major issue, seek some professional advice or coaching.

A final word about behaviour. When you communicate something important on your change initiative staff will look for consistency between your words and your behaviour not just as you talk, but after you have talked. Take a simple example. Let's say you tell everyone that it is important to come into the office on time. Then, as well as saying this, you need to be seen to be coming into the office on time, otherwise no one will take the request seriously. Mismatches between your behaviour and your words will be observed. They will generate cynicism, a loss of respect for you personally and a loss of authority.

brilliant tip

Beyond words

In this chapter, I have mostly made reference to communicating by words and by your behaviour. Words will always be the foundation stone of our communication. But there is increasing interest in visualisation techniques in the professional world. It is beyond the scope of this book to discuss such techniques, other than to say they can be powerful ways both for communicating and for engaging teams. If you are interested in exploring this further, a good source of information is *Visual Leaders: New Tools for Visioning, Management, and Organizational Change* by David Sibbert.

brilliant recap

You communicate on change initiatives to share and gather information, to develop rapport and trust, and to build support for the change.

Specific challenges with communicating on change arise from the difficulties of being open and providing information in a timely fashion. Often these problems are exaggerated. You should try to be as open as possible – it will ease future problems. If you really need to keep information secret, keep it to a limited group and try to plug any leaks. Although you may not have all the information you want, you can generally keep a stream of communications going, for example by referring to the plan.

Change communication must be a two-way process. Listening, and being seen to listen, are as important as transmitting information.

▶

When thinking about how to communicate, consider your goals, audiences, messages and channels. Do not forget the need for regular reinforcement of consistent messages.

The messages required will be specific to your change, but broadly there are four phases you should think of: communication in preparation for the change, during the change development, as the change is implemented, and after the change is complete.

To develop a communication plan think in terms of your key audiences and the main events on the change initiative. Factor into your plan the logistics and diary constraints of your stakeholders, especially senior stakeholders. You must fit around their availability; they will not fit around your plan.

Align your communications with your behaviour. Your team may notice inconsistency between your words and your body language. They will certainly notice inconsistencies between your words and your behaviour after talking. These will reduce the impact of your messages, as well as reducing your credibility.

CHAPTER 9

Arrive, sustain
and move on

What differentiates successful and unsuccessful change is how the change is sustained. While change projects come and go, the resulting change must be a permanent alteration in team behaviour and ways of working if the change is to be successful (at least until the next change). As part of the change initiative you must put the foundations in place so the change is a permanent alteration in the way the team works, and not some transient event.

This section talks about how change is sustained, when you should feel comfortable that your work in managing the change is over, and this leads onto a discussion about how you can maximise the benefit from the change project by using it as a learning opportunity. The chapter ends by reflecting on how you can contribute to making your team more flexible or adaptable to future changes.

Sustaining change

Let's assume you have executed your change plan fully. The initiative is unlikely to have gone exactly as you originally intended, but there will come a time when the tasks in the plan are completed. It can be easy to conclude that the change must be over because the tasks in the plan are finished. Unfortunately, life is not quite so simple, and this conclusion is often wrong. Change has a habit of unravelling, with old ways of working re-establishing themselves. Bedding in of new ways of working takes time, breaking old habits takes a period of concentrated effort and reinforcement. Business history has countless examples of changes which were thought complete, but which unravelled because there was no effort to sustain the change. This is sometimes referred to as 'calling victory too soon'.

In chapter 6 I introduced the plan–do–review cycle, and the way you should track progress at three levels: task, deliverable and outcome. When a plan has been completed all it shows is that all the tasks you thought you would need to do have been done. That does not guarantee that all the deliverables have been produced, nor that people are using these deliverables to achieve the outcomes expected. Before you call a stop make sure all the outputs from the initiative that you require have been produced, and that they are contributing towards the necessary outcome. Even if they are, you need to go beyond this to feel certain that this will continue once the change initiative has been stopped.

Think in terms of the field force diagram I introduced in chapter 7. Those resisting forces may be still there, and if you stop the driving forces then there is a risk the change will unravel and all will move back to where it was. An end of your initiative does not magically entail the end of any resisting forces to change. If this happens, old behaviours and old ways of working will re-emerge.

One of the most important aspects to ensure a change is sustained is consistency and alignment of the change with the other aspects of the organisation which drive performance and behaviour. I have mentioned *systemic alignment* several times through this book. Systemic alignment becomes critically important *after* the change initiative has ended. Is there anything in your team, the organisation as a whole, or the way you manage the team that is acting contrary to the spirit of the change?

There are many factors to consider. But the factors which I most often see causing issues are:

1   ***Performance management:*** one of the central mechanisms for driving behaviour in organisations is the performance management system – how you provide feedback and reward people for their performance, as well as what factors you consider in promotions. It seems obvious that if you want people to change from way of working A to way of working B, then you must start to reward B and stop rewarding A – obvious, but all the time organisations continue to reward and encourage one sort of behaviour while expecting another. This fact has been discussed for decades in management research, but still time and again there is often a misalignment between the desired behaviour and performance management systems. There is a famous and very good paper that discusses this point. It is called 'On the folly of rewarding A, while hoping for B'. It was written by Steven Kerr in 1975. It is not a long paper, and given its age it may seem a little dated. I think it is worthwhile reading for all managers who are involved in change. It is also worth sharing with others who are responsible for setting performance goals and targets. You can easily find a copy of this paper on the Web.

2   ***Behaviour:*** the next consideration is the behaviour of key influencers, such as yourself, other managers and any other influential people. As a team leader you will be watched all the time, and whatever you do that is not consistent with the change will be noticed. If you don't follow the change it gives your team members the message 'it's ok to ignore the change'. You want to be giving the message 'well even the boss is following the change, so it must be the right thing to do'. This requires some vigilance on your part as it is very easy to find yourself doing something that is in

contradiction with the spirit of the change you have just implemented.

3 *Feedback:* support the new ways with regular feedback and reinforcement to your team members, giving positive encouragement for behaviour which is aligned with the change and appropriate intervention for behaviour which is not.

4 *Conversation:* finally, just keep talking about the change. In fact, don't talk about it as a change anymore. Make it sound as if it is a normal and everyday part of the way your team works. The way you talk and what you talk about will keep staff focussed on sustaining change.

One final important tip: don't give people an unintentional opening back to the old ways of working. This is very easy to do if there are aspects of their work which give an opportunity to go back to the old ways of working. This can be avoided by:

● Stopping old approaches and making them unavailable. If you don't do this the change may unravel. As soon as practically possible remove access to old systems, take away old forms or any other parts of the old ways of working. This may seem draconian, but there will often be situations in which the old systems may be preferable to some team members of occasional use. This can easily become a habit of drifting away from the new ways of working.

● Not giving any of your team the opportunity of using old ways. For various reasons, in some situations it may not seem to be a problem to let certain individuals work in old ways after a change has been implemented. This should be avoided. The problem is that this gives everyone the impression that the change is optional. There must be no 'special cases' of individuals who can continue to work in the old ways – not even amongst your star performers.

When is the change over?

What is a successful change? That depends on the situation. Each change is different, and the context in which it happens is different. Every change should be associated with some measure of success – whether that is a performance improvement, a cost reduction, a quality gain or something else. At the start of the change think through the measurable benefit the change will deliver. There will be some changes, such as those associated with culture or behaviour, which may be hard or impossible to measure quantitatively, but these should be the minority of changes.

There is never a perfect time to bring a change initiative to an end. Bringing a change initiative to an end means releasing the people who were working on it. They may go back to their normal business-as-usual role; they may transition to a new or modified role as a result of the change; some will go on to further projects. Ideally in bringing the change to a close you can really dot the I's and cross the T's. However, this is a rare luxury. Pragmatically you must find the point at which the benefits of continuing are fewer than the benefits of releasing people to work elsewhere. A sensible priority call is made and the initiative ends. But whatever pressures you may be under to release people, try not to be too hasty.

I have seen teams on numerous occasions working sub-optimally because some aspect of a change has not been finalised. If you do need to close the change initiative down and release the team working on it then make sure you do this with an explicit understanding of any compromises being made. At the very least capture any gaps and omissions for inclusion in your next change initiative.

The end of the initiative as a formally tracked endeavour with a dedicated team may not be the end of the change. You may need to track certain outstanding actions to be picked up as part of business-as-usual work. You should track the performance metrics relevant to the change for some time before you can be certain the change is fully embedded. Stop doing this too early and you risk the change unravelling.

This leads to the question: when is the change over? When can you stop thinking about this change and move onto other projects or back to your normal work?

The answer to the first question relates to the performance measures I introduced in chapter 5. When you have achieved and can sustain the improvement in performance the change was designed for then the change is over. In reality, there will be occasions on which a change fails to deliver the expected performance improvement. Then you need to make a management decision if the change approach has delivered all it will ever deliver. Sometimes, changes over-deliver in terms of performance improvements. That is a great outcome when it happens.

Answering the second question is trickier. It requires judgement, rather than formal measurement. You are seeking a deeper answer. That deeper answer is when the change is no longer a change, when it is no longer treated as something new, but is 'just the way things are done around here'.

In practice, the time to stop the initiative as a distinct piece of work is when there are diminishing returns to ongoing work and the resources are better applied elsewhere. The time to claim success is when the benefits are being achieved. The time to halt focussing on the change is when the change is the business-as-usual way of working.

Learning

There is one important thing to do before a change initiative can be closed down and team members released. Change initiatives provide ways to drive performance improvements, and they are also ideal learning situations. Learning happens all the time, but the most profound and lasting learning happens when you take time to reflect and think about what you have gone through and consider how you will face the next change you are involved in. The learning organisation has been a goal of many for years. In your team alone you will not make this a reality, but you can at least make a contribution on the way by encouraging learning in the team.

This is really important in change because the truth is that the end point of a change initiative is frequently the beginning of the next. Change is often presented as a linear process, but it is more realistic to think of it as cyclical. Every change is an important event in its own right, but also the foundation of the next change.

There is another reason to focus on reviewing your change projects. It gives everyone involved a chance to get things off their chest. While I don't think a project review should solely be performed as a kind of group catharsis, a good review will result in some of the residual stresses and strains from the change programme being released. A well-run review ends with smiles and laughter.

In your role as a team leader, the ability to manage change should not be seen as a specialised or optional skill – it is a core skill all team leaders need. At times you may need expert change management support, but you must become comfortable with the basic elements of managing change.

Given its importance to you as a manager, you should seize the opportunity to develop your capability to manage change by learning from every change project. There are many ways to learn from projects and changes, and a simple constructive way is to think about the things you have learnt in the context of future changes:

1   On future changes what will you START to do that you did
    not do this time?

2   On future changes what will you STOP doing that you did
    this time?

3   On future changes what will you CONTINUE to do that
    you did this time?

When doing a review, just remember these three words: start–
stop–continue. Don't forget the last one. Change can be
demanding and it is easy to fall into the trap of thinking only
about mistakes. Often the best learning comes from thinking
about what went well and should be repeated. It is much more
motivating, and research shows it is often more productive to
focus on your strengths. Try to leverage them, rather than trying
to resolve all your weaknesses.

As part of pinpointing what you will continue to do, identify
and capture any reusable materials from the initiative. These
may be either to be directly reused or become examples for
future change initiatives. For instance, plans from change initiatives are rarely reusable, but they are great to refer to, to help in
identifying tasks that should be in the plan of other initiatives.
Similarly communications materials are rarely directly reusable.
But parts of them may be. I have a presentation that was used
to brief first-level team leaders on their roles during a large corporate change programme quite a few years ago. I have found
many of the slides as useful as they were on the original change
initiative on several programmes since.

Sometimes reviews can turn into exercises in finger-pointing
and assigning blame for problems that arose. That is never
productive. If censure needed to be applied, it should have been
done before the review. A review will only really work if team
members are open and honest. This will only happen if people
sense problems are not to be raised for blame, but only to learn

from. If a change initiative was large and particularly rancorous it is often worth using an external facilitator. The facilitator can run the review and ensure it is a productive session that bonds rather than causes tensions in the team.

You should not just consider learning as something for you, but as something the whole team can develop from. The best teams to lead are the ones that learn from all their experience. Take the time to learn from a change as a team, and you will find that the next time a change occurs it will be easier and less risky. People who are familiar with regular change tend to find the process of changing less difficult. If practical, it can be helpful during such a review to include one or two external stakeholders in the change who can describe what the change felt like to them.

Learning will be most likely to occur when you not only review the change, but also when you assign real actions as a result of the learning. These actions should be meaningful and tracked to ensure they are followed through.

Celebrating

The end of a change initiative is a time for saying farewells to any temporary staff and giving thanks for people's efforts and their patience. Sometimes this justifies celebration, thanking the team for all their hard work on driving the change, and recognising the effort and stress people have gone through. The celebration needs to be appropriate.

Do not underestimate the benefits of thanking people. Recognition is a powerful motivator. This is important because it is likely that fairly soon you will be asking your team to change again. So it's best to leave them with as positive an experience as possible of the current change.

Designing for future changes

What's next? Sooner or later it will be another change. Charles Darwin is often quoted as having said: 'It is not the strongest of the species that survives, nor the most intelligent that survives. It is the one that is most adaptable to change.' Actually, it's hard to find the actual source of these words and their attribution to Darwin is highly questionable. Still, it's a great quote and in the spirit of his work. It is also a good point to reflect on as we reach the end of the book.

One of the questions worth asking yourself is how do you build on the foundations in every change, so the next change can be a bit easier? Another way of putting this is: how do you make yourself adaptable to change? You want to be running the team that survives!

Flexibility, adaptability and agility are common words in managers' vocabularies. But if these words are to be anything more than lip service then you need to do something about them. A team does not become flexible, adaptable or agile because the managers of the team use those words a lot, although that does seem to be the assumption of many managers.

A team becomes flexible or agile by having adaptability designed into its components and the way it works in the first place. That means designing the components for requirements you have in the future, not just for the requirements you have now. The difficulty is that you do not know now what future requirements you will have. The answer is to develop components which are flexible to change – whatever that change might be. A simple analogy is what makes Lego such a great toy is that it is adaptable to everything a child might imagine. The bricks remain the same, but every time they are used something new and different can be built.

Back in chapter 4, I identified a list of some of the main variable aspects of your team. You can think about each one of these in terms of flexibility for future changes. For each variable aspect I have noted examples of issues related to change:

- *The organisation of the team:* does the organisation of the team ease future changes or hinder them? Can you easily reconfigure the team if you needed to, or would it be a major undertaking? Can you quickly set the team up for new projects?

- *Ways of working:* are processes, procedures and work instructions described and stored in such a way that they are easy to refer to and adapt? Are ways of working convoluted and hard to alter, or clear, simple and easy to improve?

- *Supporting tools:* are supporting tools such as IT systems rigidly inflexible or are they easy to adapt and add new functionality to? Are enhancements undertaken quickly and cheaply, or is it a major headache every time you need something improved?

- *Facilities:* are the facilities you have, such as office space, rapidly reconfigurable to new arrangements of the team or other challenges?

- *Skills:* does your team have a set of broad skills that can be applied to new situations? Is the team open to learning new skills quickly if this is required?

- *Performance management and metrics:* can you easily modify the performance management system to align performance metrics and incentives with new situations as they arise? Do your performance metrics facilitate change or encourage the status quo?

- *Relationships:* do the relationships you have help or hinder you in change? How could you adapt your relationships to have greater support with change?

- *Culture:* does your team culture welcome or reject change? How do you develop a positive change culture?

- *Location:* is your team spread in such a way that communicating and ensuring consistency of direction is simple or challenging? Are you based in jurisdictions in which it is easier or harder to implement change? Do time zones affect the ease of change?

Flexibility sometimes comes at a price, and it's difficult to build a business case to invest in flexibility at an abstract level. It must be related to a known problem or opportunity. It is unlikely you will have the time or resources to develop flexibility in every aspect of your team, but then you probably do not need to. Additionally, you may have no control over some aspects of your team – and you have no power to make them more flexible. For example, you may have limited ability to change facilities, and IT systems may be controlled at a more senior level. But this does not mean you can do nothing to improve flexibility.

Think about the last few changes you have implemented in the team. Are there any components or aspects of the team that repeatedly cause issues when it comes to change? Of these components are any under your control or do you have the ability to influence the future development of any of them? If there are, it is these areas you should think about and assess how you can redevelop them so they are more flexible in the future.

⟳ **brilliant** recap

Achieving successful change is not just a matter of running change initiatives, of completing projects or programmes. Change needs to be sustained. The long-term outcome from a change initiative will be affected by a wide range of factors in the organisation, including performance management, your behaviour, the way you give feedback and reinforcement to appropriate behaviour. This is important, and if you do not want to consider or work on these aspects of change, then your investment in change initiatives may give you no return.

Having completed a change initiative is a great opportunity for learning. Experience shows that the organisations that thrive are the ones that learn. Change will both show you things that you will want to do again, and let you experience mistakes that you want to avoid. No change initiative is perfect, but they can be perfect learning situations at an individual and team level.

A final consideration. The end point for many changes is simply the start of the next change. Some aspects of your team will be changed time and time again. If you want to be flexible and agile for future changes, it is worth looking at how you design your team and all the supporting components so they are flexible for future changes.

Good luck with all your changes.

To help you on your way, I have included a list of summary questions in Appendix 1. Next time you are running a change initiative in your team, use the following questions to help you identify your strengths and areas that need a little more focus. Refer back to this book if a particular question does not inspire you with what you need to do.

Appendix 1
Summary questions

Start from the right place (chapter 2)

- Are you starting from a good place? For example:
  - Do you understand your team's role and what the people in your team each contribute to achieving this role? Do you have a practical, current, working knowledge of the team and the context in which the team exists?
  - Do team members have appropriate job descriptions and up-to-date performance appraisals?
  - Do you have a good set of relationships within and external to the team that will support you through your change journey?
  - Do you understand the expectations and views of entitlements of team members?
  - Do you know what is in your team members' contracts?
  - Do you have the competency and capacity to undertake your desired changes?
- Is there anything you can/should do to close any gaps prior to starting your change? Or should closing the gaps be a change initiative?

Finding clarity, making clarity (chapter 3)

● Do you understand the strategy you must implement – have you *found clarity*? Do you need to *make greater clarity* for your team to have a meaningful vision?

● Do you have a vision for your team which is:

  – Believable but challenging;

  – Compelling and worthwhile to achieve;

  – Exciting to team members and will start them pondering how to achieve it;

  – Something team members associate with; and

  – Is it consistent with and a logical extension of the organisational strategy?

Identifying changes (chapter 4)

● Have you reviewed the various aspects of your team to identify parts you could improve?

● Do you have a clear idea of your change agenda? Are the individual changes prioritised relative to your change capacity?

● Have you found the right balance between:

  – Radical and evolutionary change;

  – Reactive and proactive changes;

  – Fixing faults and building on strengths;

  – Changes within the team and lobbying for changes elsewhere in the organisation?

● Have you considered how you could adapt and improve your management and leadership style as part of the change agenda?

Plan the change (chapter 5)

● Do you have a robust and flexible plan for change – with a beginning, middle, implementation and end?

   – Will this plan achieve the expected change? Does that include achieving the necessary level of performance improvement?

   – Does the plan make the best balance of time, resource, cost and risk to achieve this change?

   – Does the plan encompass all the necessary work? Are there any gaps and omissions in the plan?

   – Does the plan account for the dependencies between tasks?

   – Has the systemic alignment of this change with other components of your team (or external to your team) been thought through?

   – In planning have you considered your story and your stakeholders?

   – Are there any other external factors, such as commitments or key organisation events, that the plan needs to account for?

   – Does your plan take account of decision-maker availability and logistics?

   – Is the implementation or transition approach appropriate for this change?

   – Does this plan take a realistic view of the way your organisation works, how things get done and how long they take?

● Has the planning process enabled team members to develop a robust and shared understanding of what needs to be done?

Change and do the day job (chapter 6)

● Do you have an effective way of mobilising your team to develop and deliver the change?

● Do you have an effective plan–do–review cycle in place to do the work required, review where you are, and appropriately maintain and update the plan?

● Are the tasks being completed according to the plan – and is doing this leading to the necessary deliverables which will enable you to achieve your desired outcome?

   – Do you have a way of assessing or measuring progress towards your goal?

● Do you have a mechanism in place which you can quickly and effectively identify and resolve problems with your change initiative?

● Do you have a clear understanding of your stakeholders?

   – How will you manage their expectations about the change and about business-as-usual work during the change?

   – How will you engage and maintain relationships with the stakeholders during the change?

   – Are you focussed on a balanced set of stakeholders – both those in favour of and those resisting the change?

● Have you considered how you will keep business-as-usual running smoothly during your change programme? In particular, have you considered:

   – The capacity of the team and availability of key staff during the change?

   – How you will keep team members focussed on their normal work during the change?

   – How you will deal with any unexpected knock-on impacts of the change?

   – How you will allocate your time and focus during the

change, between the business-as-usual work and the change initiative?

● Have you planned your implementation/transition that appropriately balances the risk of impact on business-as-usual work with the speed and the cost of the change?

Adapting to and adopting change (chapter 7)

● How will you develop *awareness* and *understanding* of the change?

● What do you need to do to ensure your team members have the capability and skills to work in the way the change requires?

– Do you need any skills development or training? How will you deliver this?

– Will you be undertaking any recruitment? How will you recruit the required staff in a timely fashion?

– Will your change involve any redundancies? How will you undertake this?

● How will you encourage your team members' *willingness* to work in the new way?

– What resistance do you expect, and how do you plan to deal with it?

– Will your change challenge any existing mental models, fixed (unspoken) assumptions and default thinking? How will you handle this?

– Will your team members try to strike a bargain about the change? Will you or will you not negotiate? What is your bargaining approach?

– Have you considered how you will build and maintain belief in the change? Do you need and have any quick wins?

- How will you make use of the change curve during the change initiative?

● Do you understand the driving and restraining forces for change?

- How will you leverage the driving forces?

- How will you mitigate the restraining forces?

● Will your change contain bad news for some team members? What will be your approach to communicating this and handling the response?

● As well as the impact on individuals, have you considered the team as a whole?

- How will team members influence each other?

- What will be the effect on team performance and maturity of the change?

- How will you ensure the team does not degrade as a result of the change?

● Are you prepared in yourself for your own change journey?

Talking about change (chapter 8)

● Do you have an effective communications plan developed?

- Does this plan balance any need for secrecy with your team members' and other stakeholders' needs for timely information?

- Have you reflected on your communication goals, audiences, messages, channels and degree of reinforcement required?

- Have you developed an approach to communicate through the lifetime of the change – from breaking the initial news of the change to the change close-down?

- Is your communication plan built around your different prioritised stakeholders and the key events in the change initiative?

- Have you taken account of any senior stakeholders' logistics and availability when planning communications?
- Is your behaviour consistent with the messages you are communicating?
- Are you listening as well as talking?

Arrive, sustain and move on (chapter 9)

● Is the change being sustained? Are all the aspects of your team consistently aligned to reinforce and support the change? How will you make use of the following to sustain the change:
  - Performance metrics and rewards?
  - Your and other leaders' behaviour?
  - Feedback?
  - The language you use and the things you talk about?
● How will you know that the change is over, and old ways of working are not being re-established?
● What can you learn from this change?
  - How will you ensure that learning is really applied?
● Have you appropriately celebrated the end of the change?
● Are you building an agile team that can quickly adapt to future changes?
  - Are you designing for change?
● What's next?
  - What else can you do to ensure you are best placed to achieve the next change?

Appendix 2
The executive's role

This book is specifically targeted at team leaders working with a frontline team delivering whatever is the normal business of your organisation. It is not focussed on the senior leaders in the organisation. Senior leaders have teams, but teams that are made up mostly of other managers.

Having said this, many of the lessons in this book are applicable no matter how senior you are. There are additional challenges for executives leading change in an organisation. These challenges include the need to lead organisation-wide change initiatives, affecting large numbers of people, often in multiple locations. You probably have not one, but several change initiatives going on at once. You will normally be concerned both with delivering change, and building the capability to deliver change reliably again and again. These are subject matters in their own rights. They are topics I explore in my book *Financial Times Briefing: Change Management*.

In this appendix I want briefly to discuss a much more limited topic. How can you help the managers who work for you to find their way through their own change puzzles? Teams are the building blocks of your organisation. Driving change through the teams requires the support of your team managers. They can be your greatest advocates or they can be a major blockage to change.

Clarity

The first and most important thing you can do is to ensure the managers who work for you have a clarity of objectives. This clarity does not relate just to the current change initiative, but across all the things you are asking your team leaders to implement in their teams. One of the most common problems I come across time and again is a lack of clarity amongst team leaders about what their bosses really want, and the relative priority between different activities. It is not a matter of whether you have spoken to your team about strategy, objectives and priorities. It is about them understanding. This requires repeated emphasis, reinforcement and ongoing communication.

All managers have to juggle. You can help them understand which balls they need to keep in the air right now.

Support

The role of junior and middle managers can sometimes be a bit of a thankless task when it comes to change. Middle managers have often been accused of being resistant to change and seen as the root cause of all the organisation's problems. This can be true, but I think it is often a reflection of lazy thinking, and an unwillingness to accept that not enough has been done to attune them to change and convince or motivate them to work through it.

Middle managers are also the group that often suffers most in change. Many organisations still have their cadre of executives and their group of frontline staff. The teams that have been downsized most often are middle managers. Yet they can have the most to do during a change initiative, dealing with the nitty-gritty operational details and the direct reality of staff responses to change.

I have met some difficult middle managers in my time. People who seem to take pleasure in stalling change and who take a cynical attitude to every direction given. But they are few and far between. Many middle managers have lengthy tenures with their organisations and really do want to support doing what is best for the organisation. And this has included wave after wave of change. When you come across cynicism, it is often well founded. Not every executive push or strategic agenda has been well thought through or ended up being successful.

Additionally, the role that is expected of junior and middle managers during a period of change can be difficult. The mind-set they are expected to adopt requires them to juggle multiple, often conflicting, viewpoints – the organisation's interest, their team's interest and their personal interest. Many managers will effectively implement change that is not in their personal interest if you manage the process with care, are open about the implications of the change, treat them fairly and provide the support they need.

Apart from giving clear instructions, the executive or other senior manager can best help by providing an open door to the middle and junior managers. Try to understand their situation and difficulties. Listen to their viewpoints. Even if it comes across as moaning, it may contain important risks and issues you may not have thought about when you decided upon a strategic direction. Ideally, provide them with individual support and guidance. Treat it as part of your normal coaching and development of your team.

Often the best help for someone getting bogged down in change is simply a calm head with a few more years' experience to help them focus and not drown in change. Give some positive feedback and thanks for their efforts. Show your managers how to see their way through the maze of problems they are facing. Help them identify what are the important things to focus on and what can be left to worry about another day.

If and when you feel yourself getting impatient with what you perceive as foot-dragging from the managers who work for you, before you get irritable, take a deep breath. Sometimes a more assertive sense of direction and urgency from you can help. More ambitious targets than many middle managers expect have been shown to be achievable in project after project. But always remember you don't just want change, you want sustained change. Cutting corners and forcing things through may get you to the end of a change project more quickly. It may also result in longer-term issues with the change.

Make sure the managers are really clear about what you want and your priorities. If you are getting a lot of push-back, before you decide that this is just self-interest blocking necessary change, make sure that there are no real problems with implementing the change. Help them understand they are not fighting a battle alone.

Often executives expect other managers to take their teams on the change journey. There is an attitude that as they are managers they just have to get on with it. They are often inexperienced at managing change. To be successful, you must invest the time to support and motivate them.

Lead by example

The only other thing I want to stress, as has been repeatedly emphasised, is to lead by example. The people in your organisation will observe your behaviour, and your behaviour will set the role model for what is and is not acceptable. The more senior you are, typically the more visible and influential your behaviour will be.

If you want your teams to work in a certain way and to exhibit specific behaviours then you need to as well. The era of 'do what I say, not what I do' was over decades ago. Everyone knows this. All experienced senior managers and executives understand this point, and if asked would say it is important, but really common sense. Yet repeatedly I see senior leaders falling down on this point.

Let me give you an example. I know an executive who is always complaining about the way his staff drift into the office at various times. He is constantly telling his managers to get their teams to their desks on time. This is not him being an old-fashioned control freak. His teams provide a vital operational role for the organisation and it is one of those roles that still needs to be done by people at local desks. Customers expect 24-hour service, and the operational functions need to support this. So his complaints have a reasonable grounding, and what he is trying to achieve is essential for the smooth operation of the business.

What he never accounts for is that he often does not arrive before 11. There are several reasons for this. He has a busy schedule and often works late. He travels regularly on business and has to give up weekends. There is no doubt he puts in the hours. He is also not directly doing a hands-on operational role, so the specific hours he works or the location he works from should be less relevant. From the perspective of him simply performing his executive function there is no problem with him arriving at 11. But this misses the point. The example he sets is interpreted to mean that drifting in late is ok. He visibly and regularly comes into the office around 11. While he does this, he will always be fighting an uphill battle to get the rest of the team in on time.

Leading by example does not need to be hard. It is not about being perfect. It simply requires you to take some care, to reflect on how you act and to try and ensure it is aligned with the spirit of the changes you are implementing. If you are unsure about what to do, try to get some feedback from someone you trust and who will be open with you. Find out how your personal behaviour affects the people who work in your teams.

Appendix 3
Increasing your knowledge and getting help

I have drawn inspiration from a number of sources in writing this book. Most obviously I have drawn on the increasingly mature body of knowledge that makes up change management. Change management is becoming a well-established discipline with its own qualifications, accreditations and community of practitioners. After reading this book you may decide you want to find out more. In this appendix I provide some tips towards increasing your own knowledge and where to go for help.

Books and references

A great reference for anyone who wants a broad and deep understanding of change management is the Change Management Institute's *Change Management Body of Knowledge* or CMBoK.

There are many other good change management books. One of the most influential writers on change management for many years has been John Kotter. In his book *Leading Change* he provides a clear and widely applied eight-stage process for managing change, which is widely referenced by managers and executives. If you are looking for a broader overview of change management theories and tools a good text is Cameron and Green's *Making Sense of Change Management*. If you prefer a more academic coverage of change management a very comprehensive book is Hayes' *The Theory and Practice of Change Management*.

Elsewhere in this book (in chapters 5 and 8), I have also referred to two books which, while not directly change management books, provide very helpful ways of thinking and tools for change. They are:

The Fifth Discipline: The Art and Practice of the Learning Organization by Peter Senge.

Visual Leaders: New Tools for Visioning, Management, and Organizational Change by David Sibbert.

This is meant as a practitioner book, but there are several ground-breaking academic pieces of research I have referred to (in chapters 7, 8 and 9). While they are all relatively old, the thinking in them remains important and influential. They vary in terms of how accessible and easy they are to read, and they are widely quoted in books and secondary literature. But if you are the type of person who likes to read the originals, they are:

'On the folly of rewarding A, while hoping for B', Steven Kerr.

On Death and Dying, Elisabeth Kübler-Ross, MD.

Defining the 'Field at a Given Time', Kurt Lewin.

Nonverbal Communication and *Silent Messages: Implicit Communication of Emotions and Attitudes*, Professor Albert Mehrabian.

Developmental Sequence in Small Groups, Bruce Tuckman.

I have written three other books specifically on change management. One is aimed at the executive community; one is a practical approach to structuring a change programme; and one is aimed to provide a comprehensive combination of project, programme and change management with links to other disciplines such as strategy development and business analysis. In order, they are:

Financial Times Briefing: Change Management.

Managing Change Step-by-Step.

The Practice and Theory of Project Management, Delivering Value through Change.

Links to other disciplines

For many people it will be obvious that I have drawn on *project management* thinking in this book. My first profession was as a project manager, and most of my work requires calling on project and programme management. *Programme management* has more of a focus on change and running change initiatives. There are bodies in different countries which promote professionalism in project management such as the APM in the UK and the PMI in the US.

As a team leader some knowledge of project and programme management is very helpful, but I do not think you need to be an expert. Much team-based change is sufficiently complex and risky that applying project management principles and practices is advisable. But once you get beyond the sort of change that can be delivered with a relatively basic understanding of project management you are probably better off calling on a professional project manager than doing it yourself. However, if you do want to learn more about project management there are numerous good books and courses available.

As well as change and project management this book also draws on my experience, and years of reading and education, in management and leadership. As I hope I have shown, while change management is a distinct discipline, successful change builds on good management and leadership practice. Much of the development you undertake as a team leader will help you in change situations.

Internet resources

There is a huge range of Web-based resources, which change faster than a printed book can keep up with. A quick search under the words 'organisational change' or 'change management' will throw up a huge variety of information. It is worth doing this if you are looking for tools, templates or ideas. But as with so much on the internet, filtering the wheat from the chaff can be a prolonged exercise!

If you like my writing then you can find a library of my articles and follow my blog at **www.changinghats.co.uk**.

Advisers and consultants

Consultants have a useful role to play in change, either by giving extra capacity to your team or by providing specialist expertise. All the major management consultancies, and many of the minor ones, provide change management expertise as part of their normal service or as a specialisation.

The first challenge with consultants is having sufficient budget to engage them. The second challenge is selecting the right consultants for you. I am going to focus on the second in this section. Depending on your seniority you may have more or less influence over the choice of professional advisers.

There are differences in capabilities and focus between consultancies. For delivery of sustained change use advisers with in-depth expertise in implementation and delivery. Irrespective of which company is your favoured professional service provider, when you select help for a particular initiative it is the capabilities of the specific individuals who come and work with you and not the track record of the firm that matters. Do not be fobbed off with junior staff who will be overseen by an experienced partner or senior manager – if you want to minimise risk use individuals with a proven track record. Change is not purely about technical skills, it is about understanding people. This type of understanding tends to come with experience.

I am a consultant, but I strongly recommend you avoid the trap of thinking that consultants are essential to successful change. They can be helpful to speed up your initiative and reduce risk. Outsiders can be powerfully useful in challenging complacency and seeing beyond the 'givens' of a business. Search around and you will find consultants who have experiences in situations which are very similar to yours. But rarely are consultants indispensable.

Whatever you do, you retain accountability for delivery of change. Consultants can help, but they should never have total responsibility for the change. Too great a dependency on consultants can, over time, limit your own change management capabilities. They may also not understand some of the intangible aspects of the fabric of your organisation.

If you do involve consultants, try to ensure that your own staff learn from the process. Don't leave the change initiative under the sole control of the consultants. Make skills transfer to your staff part of the success criteria for the consultants. When you develop your change initiative plans, ensure they contain realistic transition plans to move away from the consultants by a predefined phase of the initiative.

If you are short of resources, one alternative is to recruit interim managers to perform business-as-usual roles and free up key staff to run the change themselves. This may seem risky, but if your team and processes are well designed and running smoothly, this can be less risky than delegating a change initiative to outsiders with a relatively short-term focus and limited understanding of your business.

Courses and accreditation

If change is a regular part of your work you may want to consider studying it or gaining a change management accreditation – or encouraging someone in your team to do this. Change management is becoming an increasingly mature discipline, and the Change Management Institute (see Appendix 4) currently provides two levels of accreditation.

Most MBA courses have modules on change management, and many business schools run shorter courses specifically focussed on change or transformation. Additionally, professional bodies such as the CIPD and Chartered Management Institute in the UK provide change management courses and lectures. These can provide a powerful basis to assist in delivering change and forums to discuss and share experiences. Some insights from experts can make significant differences to the success of a change initiative.

In the end, change management is a practical discipline and even the best course is never a complete replacement for experience.

Appendix 4
Join the community

The Change Management Institute

If you are interested in change management and want to become part of the wider community of practitioners then why not join the Change Management Institute?

The Change Management Institute is a not-for-profit professional organisation. Membership is open to anyone with an interest in change management, particularly supporting change managers to grow and develop in their chosen career by providing credibility, connectivity and capability. For further information please go to the CMI website at **www.change-management-institute.com**.

The Change Management Institute encourages networking between change managers, runs seminars and provides accreditation. It also develops and maintains the Change Management Body of Knowledge or CMBoK.

Keeping in touch

I am a regular contributor to blogs and magazines. I keep a library of my articles, many of which are relevant to change management available and free to access online at **www.changinghats.com**. I also maintain a blog on the same site. You can also follow me on Twitter at @RJNtalk, where I flag when I have written a new article or updated the blog.

At the date of publication, I am the author of 10 other books, which have been translated into 16 languages. My books can be broadly grouped under the theme of 'getting things done' – for individuals, teams or large organisations. My books try to make the complex accessible and relevant to practical realities. The books range from junior managers' guides, through executive handbooks, to academically orientated textbooks. I have also written for the non-professional market. My books include: *The Project Management Book*; *The Management Consultant: Mastering the Art of Consultancy*; *Financial Times Briefing: Change Management*; as well as the award-winning *The Management Book* (Management Book of the Year 2013).

What did you think of this book?

We're really keen to hear from you about this book, so that we can make our publishing even better.

Please log on to the following website and leave us your feedback.

It will only take a few minutes and your thoughts are invaluable to us.

www.pearsoned.co.uk/bookfeedback

Index